THE
ISOLATED
Variable

THE
ISOLATED
Variable

TIMOTHY GRAY

TATE PUBLISHING
AND **ENTERPRISES**, LLC

Published by Tate Publishing & Enterprises, LLC
127 E. Trade Center Terrace | Mustang, Oklahoma 73064 USA
1.888.361.9473 | www.tatepublishing.com

Tate Publishing is committed to excellence in the publishing industry. The company reflects the philosophy established by the founders, based on Psalm 68:11,
"The Lord gave the word and great was the company of those who published it."

Book design copyright © 2016 by Tate Publishing, LLC. All rights reserved.
Cover design by Niño Carlo Suico
Interior design by Gram Telen

Published in the United States of America

ISBN: 978-1-68207-706-1
Biography & Autobiography / Personal Memoirs
15.12.15

Introduction

Evelyn Waugh wrote a book that was published in 1957 called *The Ordeal of Gilbert Pinfold*. This is the note that appears at the beginning of the book:

> Three years ago Mr. Waugh suffered a brief bout of hallucination closely resembling what is here described. It was an interesting experience for a man whose business is story-telling. Hallucination is far removed from loss of reason. The reason works with enhanced power, while the materials for it to work on, presented by the senses, are delusions. A story-teller naturally tries to find a plot into which his observations can be fitted.
>
> Much that was tediously repetitive has been omitted. Nothing of importance has been added. Mr. Waugh does not deny that "Mr. Pinfold" is largely based on himself. Subsidiary characters are fictitious.
>
> Since his disconcerting voyage he has learned that a great number of sane people suffer in this way from time to time. He believes this record may amuse them.

The "hallucination" that takes center stage in *The Isolated Variable* is what I heard while alone in my apartment in January of 2011: "You treat me like I've got green polka dots." If it was really a hallucination, I guess I must marvel at how witty I can be with myself. I wrote the book under the premise that it was not a hallucination, until the time comes toward the end when I must admit that I had been at least partly delusional.

Even if I'm wrong, however, about all of my "delusional" beliefs, I feel, like Evelyn Waugh, that my book has value. Perhaps my ambitions are such that I strain for more than a hope to only "amuse." The part of my "delusions" that I wind up conceding are false don't necessarily rule out the possibility of my center-stage "hallucination" being real. I consider the part that I concede to be false to have been disproved. I guess what is so seductive about the whole thing is that so much of it cannot presently be disproved, which of course puts it in the category, according to some, of a "self-reinforcing delusion" or a "fixed, false belief."

What I find to be so profound about Evelyn Waugh's note is the point about such an affliction being any but a *loss* of reason. Again, if the whole stack of cards that my mind has created is really only in my mind, I must marvel at the complexity of it all, and I must agree that reason has been working with "enhanced power."

Preface

In the fall of 1991, I was attempting to finish my last year at a big state university. My psychiatrist's office was in Birmingham, Michigan—close to Bloomfield Hills. My university was several states away, so I was flying back to Michigan once a month to see the shrink.

The little paragraph I just wrote sounds innocuous enough. There was a time when I would not have thought twice about what the paragraph states. But now I think back on the time in question, and I see a panther about to leap upon its prey. Now it seems to me that the paragraph above is, comparatively speaking, like a paper cartoon cat snipped out of the funny section of a newspaper. It describes what was happening to my physical body in 1991 but does not begin to take into account what was happening at the time.

"What was happening" in 1991, at least my perception of it, was almost completely confined to my own head. My shrink was encouraging me to ask a certain someone out on a date. That is the paper thin version of what was happening.

I was protesting that my heart belonged to someone else from whom I was separated by an ocean. He was trying to persuade me to consider being interested in two girls at the same time, something about which I had been quite stringent throughout my young life. I was 22 years old at the time. Both romantic interests were tenuous at best when it comes to even the paper thin version of reality. The girl I was talking to him about, the one he wanted me to date, did not have any interest in dating me.

"What was happening" during my seventh semester at university—September to December, 1991—was *nearly* confined to my own head. I occasionally imagined some kind of correlation between the cheap book propped up in my dorm room about the sensationalist pop singer, Madonna, and what was on display at the university library—Madonna's picture somehow associated with the deterioration of paper. I guess the library's obscure point holds since I now feel the need to describe the once-famous celebrity as a sensationalist pop singer. My perception of a correlation between what was displayed at the library and what I had on display in my dorm room constitutes what I consider to be a hiccup—a departure from the paper thin version of reality within which my body was moving.

Another instance of some pulp being thrown into the mix of what was usually, or overtly, dry and thin reality has its roots in an introduction to psychology class I took as a freshman at the same university. The professor was addressing a lecture hall full of five hundred students, but he seemed to direct unusual eye contact toward me. Sometimes he seemed to be staring at me as though to make a point. Four years earlier, as a freshman in high school, I'd noticed similarly unusual eye contact from one of my teachers. He also seemed to be trying to make a point. So during my seventh semester at the university, I remember seeing my old freshman year professor walking past the library. I immediately yelled out, "Science of behavior!" He stopped dead in his tracks and slowly looked around until he caught sight of me. Then he stood quietly at attention as though awaiting instructions. I got a sheepish grin on my face and turned to go, releasing him—or so it seemed. He had instructed his freshman class, on the last day of class, that if they ever saw him on campus in the years ahead, they were to yell out, "Science of behavior," which is the definition of psychology.

When I say that the first paragraph of this, my third book, calls to my mind a panther about to leap upon its prey. I don't mean that my psychiatrist was the panther in this case, or that he was the prey. I am invoking *the big picture*. I've noticed, however, that when I've become grandiose in my first two books, I'm really making my feelings into a forceful statement for my own sake, not because it is terribly helpful to my readers.

Writing two autobiographical books mostly "for my own sake" strikes some people as a great way to waste a lot of time. But I was vindicated on this point in my own eyes when I had the books ready and waiting to be read by the woman who is to become my wife in less than two months. With the book I'm writing now, I hope to leave behind and reject the sensation of being somehow in opposition to my reader. One woman gave me some feedback after I'd shown her the first draft of book number one. She said that the audience seems to be myself. How can I be in "opposition to my reader" if that reader is myself? Welcome to my world.

The idea—for books number one *and* two—was to hope and pray for a time when the world came all the way round and believed the same things about the last fifty years as I do, and did. But since this was not the case at time of composition, I considered myself to be the one reader I could count on to *understand* what the hell I was writing about. I was obliged to regard anyone else catching a glimpse of the manuscript as opposition. It is almost as if I were tapping away at a computer keyboard, seeing my words appear on the computer screen, getting to the end of a book and then losing all the composition due to a power failure. The difference is that I retain a few copies of books one and two—I just don't know what to do with them.

The difference is that the elusive characterization of myself that I seem so determined to sketch in books one and two has been eclipsed by what my future wife already sees in me, even before the world comes "all the way round" and believes something similar to what I do. When I say,

"You're in love with Clark Kent," she says, "I'm in love with Timothy Gray."

Much angst has accompanied this concept of self and its stubborn refusal to settle into a world that casts it in such humble dimensions of obscurity. One clear way the angst affected me was by deteriorating what was once very good posture. While writing book number two, my shoulders rolled more and more forward in my computer chair, and my head and neck craned themselves ever closer to the screen. This behavior had originated with book number one but got worse. The desk holding my computer had been dubbed by my father, "Command central," because it was so large and was shaped exactly like a stealth bomber and because of my tendency to become so grandiose when I thought about my impact on the world.

I lived for nine years in an apartment whose space was dominated by the command central desk. I consider it full of symbolism that I am getting rid of the desk before moving into my future wife's apartment. Starting this book, book number three, is also full of meaning for me, so it is appropriate that it nearly coincides with the date of my wedding because I am starting a new life in addition to changing my domicile. This new life derives more and more of its energy from what can be found in the present rather than from what has happened in the past, or what can be hoped for from the future.

My mother becomes distressed when she hears me refer to my life without grandiosity as a hollow shell. She maintains that my first book is not really an autobiography because it only deals with one aspect of my life. The book I'm writing now is a response to my mother's perspective.

1

In the movie, *Getting It Right*, Gavin says to Harry, Winthrop, and Jenny: "Why don't we go to a film?" Winthrop replies, "Do let me die of excitement." This kind of sarcastic reply enters the minds of many people, I have found, when someone suggests an evening to be spent at the cinema. I have firsthand experience, as an adolescent, taking a girl to the movie called *The Karate Kid*. This was in 1987, so I'm remembering the original, not the remake. It was a first date, and I didn't say anything to the girl throughout the show. It is generally true that people viewing a movie at the cinema leave as soon as the show is over. They don't linger to view the credits.

Imagine then, for a moment: One leaves the cinema, in 1991, at the end of a movie called *Little Man Tate*, and hears a twenty-two-year-old man seated in the middle of the theater—sobbing his guts out because he has been so moved by the film. That was me—crying after the movie I saw during my seventh semester at my big state university. I had walked several miles away from campus in combat boots to get to the theater. It seemed to me that the movie-goers filing past me toward the exit were interested in what they were perceiving. My impression was not that these people thought they had spotted a celebrity, or that they looked on me as larger than life. It was rather that they seemed to be honestly wondering what I was crying about, what was on my mind. They seemed to want to *know* me. They seemed to be curious as to what it was about the film they'd just seen that had brought me to such effusion.

The irony is that I was wondering the same thing: Why was I so racked with heaving waves of weeping? What came to my conscious mind, what was at the forefront of my mind, was that I was more fragile—then—than I had been previously, that the "nervous breakdown" I'd experienced just over a year earlier had left me that way, a shadow of myself.

My self-concept at the time was characterized by harsh, scathing criticisms of just about everything having to do with who I was, as is all too typical of the very young. *Little Man Tate* is about a very bright child's love for his mother. I had written a little story a few years before that was an indictment of my mother. So the second layer of my consciousness undoubtedly attributed the flood of tears in the cinema to an innate desire for reconciliation with my mother, whom I loved. I was not ostensibly estranged from my mother, and did not perceive myself to be—when it came to the first layer of consciousness—but this first layer was coming up seriously short in its attempt to explain the tears. Just about the only thing I can say that I was *always* conscious of at this time was that my mind had multi-layers of consciousness.

During this seventh semester, I was watching a lot of television. I somehow managed to get a 3.0 grade point average—that was the good news I received in the mail when I was back home with my parents in Michigan during my Christmas break. I'd gotten an *A* from one of my English professors who went out of his way to make sure that I was treated like a "senior," like I deserved respect for having made it through three years of undergraduate work, regardless of the fact that there had been a twelve-month gap in my schooling, regardless of the fact that I'd started semester number seven on academic probation. I worked with him on a few essays covering Shakespeare plays, and he categorized the work as independent study. It did not count as credit toward my English major—with which I never graduated because I left campus suddenly to return to Michigan two-thirds of the way through semester number eight.

The woman who is to become my wife one month from now tells me that I speak with educated precision, that I speak with precise compassion. The development of this attribute formed an inverse ratio with the amount of television I watched. As I watched less and less TV, I became able to be more articulate and began to enjoy public speaking more and more. Preparing a speech, however brief, I found to be much more closely linked to composition such as a writer accomplishes, rather than linked to what an actor does when he is performing on stage or in front of the camera. This was a welcome discovery. But as Henry Blackaby states, "Truth is never discovered. It is always revealed."

I was living in a dormitory in the fall of 1991, and the cafeteria plan did not provide dinners on Sundays. I routinely walked to a popular restaurant and dined on an appetizer there. It was toasted ravioli. As I left the dorm group on my way to the restaurant, I can remember wearing my new leather jacket that I'd bought on sale. It had been on sale probably because it had cloth cuffs that didn't figure to wear well. Customers had probably concluded that the cuffs would become dirty all too quickly. As I am composing at the moment, on September 2, 2011, I can say with pride that the jacket stills hangs in my closet and that the cuffs still look fine twenty years later.

New leather jacket notwithstanding, I didn't feel at all like I was standing out from the crowd, or garnering attention from girls on campus—what little I got was perfunctory. I was feeling quite aimless at times, as I questioned to myself *why* I wanted to get off academic probation, what job my English degree was going to get me. My English professor must have made sure that I was able to enjoy senior status when it came to registering for semester number eight because I remember having no trouble getting the classes I wanted.

Among those classes I registered for, those I was planning to take during semester number eight, were swim for conditioning, ballroom dancing, and an American literature class called the Rise of Realism.

Throughout my seventh semester, I was interacting on occasion with a young, black, female graduate student who seemed to hold me in profound contempt, but not so much so that she stopped interacting with me. To this day I believe she was an agent for the FBI, largely because the only moments she was ever happy in my presence, during the school year 1991–1992, were when I was slowly pulling out an envelope from my knapsack, intending to give the parcel to Amiri Baraka, who was visiting the university in the spring of 1992. He had been signing his books in a little room prior to giving a bombastic speech later that day. I never gave the envelope to Baraka, but my normally contemptuous acquaintance seemed to scamper out of the room, elated that she finally had something to report to her superiors besides, "He likes to watch tennis on television."

Why would the FBI be keeping tabs on me? My conscious mind might have attributed it to the fact that I had been put under hypnosis in Quantico, Virginia, during the twelve months I had been away from academia, and I had no idea what I said while in this state. Perhaps the level of consciousness that was most at the forefront of my mind was occupied with criticizing myself for having the idea that the woman was an agent at all, for letting such a thought even enter my head.

Another time such a thought entered my head was during semester number eight, when I was taking a bus trip from campus to a metropolis a few hours away. The bus was pulling into an airport, and I remember being galvanized as I suddenly went from a standing position to having my face pressed against the bus window. I thought I recognized the driver of a vehicle. This driver seemed to notice my face against the window, and he immediately thrust up his hand to hide his face from the other passengers on the bus.

That was my impression of what happened anyway. I would call it another hiccup, a departure from thin, dry reality—except that semester number eight was replete with such impressions and experiences. It was semester seven that was such a drag to live through. The 3.0 grade point average occasioned my being taken off academic probation. I received that news at the midpoint of the year, between semesters. The significance of no longer being on academic probation for semester eight was that my good standing put me back on the road to graduation—which meant that I had something to lose.

At some point in my time at the state university, I dropped a political science lecture and its accompanying lab component after attending only a few classes. The lecture component was held in a large auditorium while the lab occurred in a room with about thirty students, most of them young freshmen, or so it seemed to me. In the lab, I found myself defending the position, in debate, that abortion should be illegal. One student made the point that people should be able to decide for themselves what is right and what is wrong. I got really intense and said, "I can take a knife and kill you. To me, it's right. What stops me? The law." The TA in charge of the lab then started grilling me on how I proposed to deal with all the unwanted babies, etc. I didn't go any further with the argument. The students in the room were clearly horrified by what I had said. One freshman girl involuntarily pulled her skirt down a little more, while seated in her desk, as though she was afraid of me.

At lab session number two, the TA asked his students: "What is political power?" After a short exchange between the TA and a student, I said, "What you just did is an example of political power. She wanted to say something about the abortion issue, and you squelched what she said because it didn't fit into the plan you had for today's class session. You exercised the political power you hold over us, your students." He said, "That's right." At the next class session, the TA immediately gave his students an assignment. He told us to write an essay answering this question: "Was Marx right?" I didn't write a word but rather dropped the class just as immediately.

In the movie, *Getting It Right*, Gavin is cutting hair and laments that should he be without Jenny, his "junior," the clients "would all wind up looking like Harpo Marx." A few months ago, I wanted to write a poem about the gift given to me by the woman who is now my wife. At the time, I made this attempt:

> 13 years of sorrow
> Were layered internecine
> The touch of my hands
> The touch of my fingertips
>
> Etched upon my keyboard
> Etched upon the keyboard
> A keyboard that had seen
> Had been a conduit
> For what amounted to transcription
> Had seen my two books written
> My darling came across the keyboard
>
> As someone new to my life
> She set upon the task
> With Q-tips and Windex
> Of removing the sign of all those years of sorrow
>
> She absorbed the years of sorrow
> The energy radiating up and out and through
> She absorbed with her labor of love

I was not happy with this first attempt, in part because I was composing amid several conversations going on around me, and even with people interrupting me outright because they wanted to talk to me. I persevered, however, and tried again—under the same conditions and in the same situation:

> I never saw a stroke
> Never witnessed what she did
> What resulted: a clean computer keyboard
> She never witnessed firsthand
> The thirteen years of sorrow
> That keyboard had absorbed
> She went at it with Q-tips and Windex
> And removed the sign
> What had been layered and layered over the years
> The keyboard, the conduit
> Channeling my thoughts
> Forming two books that told two tales
> That told one tale
> The keyboard never witnessed
> Firsthand
> The ordeal I went through
> The keyboard absorbed
> Later
> My mind reviewing what had happened
> And recasting
> With self-expression
> Born of time to reflect
> And lend some objectivity
> To a subjective experience
>
> My love absorbed

By cleaning the keyboard
What went into those thirteen years of remembering
The keyboard had absorbed
What went into those years comprising my ordeal
The intermediate tier is the keyboard
And now it is clean!
I am free from the residue
And the sorrow
And the pain

I was ready to dispose of both these attempts when my wife asked to see them and later asked permission to try to blend them and glean from them what she could envision as the elements of a final version of the poem.

It is difficult to express how much it pleased me when my wife salvaged my two attempts and recast the ideas, the little story, of which she was one of the principal players. It was her "labor of love," so why shouldn't she have a hand in how it was put into poetry? It was she who "absorbed" the energy coming off my keyboard, she who cleaned the thing until it was new again.

Today she watched me make some progress toward decorating our Christmas tree. It is only October 22, 2011—a bit early, I suppose. I told her that the last time I had enjoyed decorating a Christmas tree was when I was eight years old. I turn forty-three next month. To return to my touchstone year, 1991, I can say that before I began my seventh semester at university, I had visited my sister in New York City for the entire month of May. I called a friend who'd been originally struck with a solo I sang in 1985, in a church with great acoustics, and read to him some of my journal entries describing my month with my sister and brother-in-law, who had not yet reached their second wedding anniversary and could still be termed newlyweds. My friend said that he'd like to read the entries I write when I am a newlywed. Perhaps this book, in addition to being a response to my mother's distress, is also a response to my friend's fervent wish and prayer that I marry the woman God had picked out for me.

2

In the movie, *Getting It Right*, Harry tells Gavin: "If you added up all the things you thought you couldn't live with, then there'd be no one left for you to live with. You can't love by a process of elimination!" If someone had told me a year and a half ago that I was about to meet a woman who would be excited about finishing one of my poems for me, I would have felt a phenomenon going on in my brain that I could only have categorized by remembering my life as an eight-year-old. The process of elimination operating for most of my life can be described as having almost completely eliminated *myself* from the running.

This act of elimination might strike one as peculiar if one considers only the current dossier, which implies that I am quite preoccupied with myself. One might conclude that herculean discipline was required for me to willingly withdraw from significant romance from age eight right up until my forty-second birthday. In fact, one might infer that discipline of that sort is incompatible with the kind of self-absorption I've supposedly experienced in recent years. To go back to my touchstone year, it was during semester number eight that two women in a karaoke bar in Michigan saw fit to try to humiliate me by singing Carly Simon's masterpiece, "You're So Vain," both staring into my eyes during the entire song. It was my entrance, apparently, and probably the way I was treating the attractive woman I was with, that had moved the two women to act with such conviction.

Perhaps what had also set off the ire of the two women was my request from the guy coordinating the singing that I be allowed to sing a couple stanzas of a song I had written instead of a song from the list of established selections. The guy never got the idea, or perhaps he was just rejecting my attempt, so I gave up and joined my date and the other couple we were with. I remember singing softly to my date, while she was driving me home, the stanzas I had wanted to sing at the karaoke bar.

I guess it is technically true that I was preoccupied with myself, that from ages nine to thirty-six I suffered from an affliction. If it can possibly be construed this way, I had a selfless duty to be concerned with myself. It was selfless in the sense that I wound up back in the home of my parents in the spring of 1992 with no plans and no money. What had been motivating me and forming the underpinnings of my decisions got me absolutely no immediate gain or reward. All I could take with me was the slightly self-absorbed conclusion that I had just accomplished something great, that the world was going to be a better place due to what the Lord God Almighty had accomplished through me, the piece of pottery.

I suppose that what I have so far of this book reflects the fact that I am rather defensive about writing about myself, writing another autobiographical book, a third book filled primarily with vignettes from my own memory. I strike out in what might seem to be the opposite direction. I am afraid of seeming self-absorbed, so I begin book number three even more wrapped up in my own mind than on the previous two occasions, the previous two beginnings.

It is all by way, however, of orientation. One can't see how glorious the new beginning is unless one has some idea of what has come before. And what cries out from books one and two is that I was lonely, that I had no one with whom to share my pain and in whom I could confide. I'm not speaking only of a spouse, though knowing and being married to my wife has made a thunderous difference in my life, but I'm referring instead to the feeling of being "crazy." I'm referring to the times my stomach sank as I sensed the deflation in the face of my listener, sensed it even while talking on the phone.

What feels odd to me is that the span, the duration of time, from when I was age nine to age twenty-three, is shorter and smaller than the span from age twenty-three to forty-three, which is my present age. Perhaps it is because I was physically growing and going through adolescence during the fourteen-year span. With all the physical changes I remember, maybe the years appear in my mind for that reason as more hectic and full of incident. In other ways, however, the twenty-year period from twenty-three to forty-three saw me developing, even seemingly deteriorating at times, which made it at least as tumultuous as the years of physical maturation.

My twenties, for example, were replete with times in which the eight-year-old inside me seemed to be struggling to reappear. The dominant consciousness of who I was had been driven underground at age nine and remained submerged throughout my teenage years. It is my current perspective on my past that my brain couldn't handle, in my twenties, this resurgence and resurfacing of the most indelible version of who I am. The eight-year-old found himself suddenly in a man's body, stronger, taller, virile, and awakening to just how successful the adult version of himself had become. It was too much for him to handle.

With the help of high doses of medication, in my mid thirties, the eight-year-old surfaced, and this time, it held. What I have been struggling to do, since that appearance on July 18, 2005, is to grow up. Today is November 26, 2011. I have had over six years to grow from age eight to whatever age the dominant consciousness is right now. I'm sure I'm much too close to what I am examining to venture a guess as to what my virtual age is at the moment. It is not that one layer of consciousness is too close to another.

I mean, rather, that I'm too close in time to the present moment, that I need at least a few weeks, sometimes more, before I can look with any kind of accuracy at what is going on in my mind.

My wife has just convinced me to delete three paragraphs. I told her in jest that I reserve the right to write badly at times. I just hope that I will always be able to recognize what needs to be deleted. The psychiatrist, Daniel Fisher, said, "The mentally ill have undergone an interruption in their social and emotional development." To understate it, one could say that I have not experienced a normal adulthood. Rather, I have been trying to mature and grow, starting at age thirty-six, from the renewed eight-year-old that was inside to whatever my virtual age is now.

To switch, for a moment, from the touchstone year of 1991, I am reminded of an incident that occurred in 1997, when I was twenty-eight years old. I was living with my parents but had purchased my own automobile a couple years before. I was driving from my home to a neighboring city, alone, when I suddenly became aware that a police car was behind me on the road, that the lights from the police car had been flashing unheeded by me for some time. I'm not sure how I could be both conscious of the time I had been apparently ignoring the car *and* somehow deadened when it came to responding to the flashing lights when I first saw them, but nevertheless, I pulled over.

The policeman was quite agitated, thinking he had been chasing a sinister culprit, asking me if there were any syringes or needles in the pockets of my leather jacket—as he checked for weapons. I kept repeating that I was a minister's son, on my way to a movie, that I simply had a tendency to "overfocus" and get lost in thought while driving. I got a ticket for speeding.

The movie I saw that night was called *The Game*. It was after seeing this movie that it first occurred to me: The "paranoia" *I* had been experiencing may also be afflicting the man I will refer to as my nemesis, but to an exponential level. However, while my "symptoms" involved grandeur, his must be about persecution. And worst of all for him, I didn't think the symptoms in either case could be characterized as *symptoms* at all.

One might interject, at this point, "No, son, that last conclusion is worst of all for *you*." What fits more easily into a self-reinforcing delusion than the conception in one's mind of what *might* be happening to one's nemesis? All I can say is that the same thought occurred to me, and I semi-successfully stuffed the eight-year-old down into the box for eight more years, until July 18, 2005.

I've heard it said that the difference between truth and fiction is that fiction must make sense. At times I am perplexed at the prospect of writing this third autobiographical book, because I am determined to avoid interpretation of the "evidence." For more than two decades, I have been in the business of connecting the dots in my mind and building what I've experienced into a framework that is solid and can survive the skepticism of the people around me. Formerly, however, I've thought of the structure as a house of cards. If one took out just one card, if the point revealed that I was wrong about anything, then the entire thing fell down, and I was back to square one.

My fervent prayer in the spring of 1996 was, "Lord, if I'm wrong about all this, please banish the thoughts forever from my mind. If I'm right, please let me retain the conviction in my mind that I am in fact right." The main argument in my mind at the time that went against the possibility of my being "right" was the sheer complexity of what being right implied. Gil Scott-Heron wrote in 1970: "The Revolution Will Not Be Televised." It was intoxicating to me, the thought that I could have had a hand in carrying the "revolution" forward, even if the news of what I did never appeared on morning TV. I saw a movie called *Bulworth* during what I refer to as my re-mission, at the end of which Amiri Baraka, playing a homeless vagrant, makes an impassioned plea into the camera: "You can't be a ghost, you got to be a *spirit!*"

I've been saying recently that I was never really all that self-absorbed, but rather I was lonely. I'd like to think that, if I suffered from anything other than loneliness, it was not self-absorption but rather self-aggrandizement. It is partly the goal of this book to put my contribution more into the context of the work of others.

3

I had a counselor maybe a decade ago who suggested that I'd lived my life up to that point "mostly within my own head." I had been a member of an advocacy group for a decade before very recently resigning. What had occasioned my resignation was learning, firsthand, the difference between advocacy, which involves being supportive, and activism, which involves doing something to right a wrong. I consider the steps I took as an activist, only one of which was resigning, to be indicative of the behavior of someone who no longer lives mostly within his own head.

My behavior during the spring semester, semester number eight, at my big state university in 1992 was unlike what had come during the previous passive semester, semester number seven, when my main objective was only to register for semester eight classes and get off academic probation. During semester eight, academics took a distinct nosedive when it came to my priorities and was replaced by whatever my instincts were telling me I should be doing at the time. The validity of my judgment also takes a nosedive, in most people's minds, when I admit that I stopped taking my antipsychotic medication in December, right before semester eight started. My credibility, therefore, is not worth much in most people's eyes when I maintain that I prayed fervently to God as to whether I should take the medication and sensed that I shouldn't, at least not at that particular time.

It was not only people's perception of this decision that has eroded my credibility over the years. Midway through my second book, I describe my contrition and the process of repentance. One sentence goes: "My life needs to take off in a new direction, with a new emphasis and, at the same time it needs to be anchored firmly to what's important." That is exactly what happened in my life. I'm reminded of what Marius sings in the musical, *Les Miserables*, about meeting Cosette: "And yet, with you my world has started." I can no longer make the audacious claim that I am the only developed character in my writing. My wife has grounded the charge of electricity.

I no longer feel that I am in opposition to my reader, and yet I must admit that in recent months, when I bring up a point in conversation that I consider to be evidence of a groundswell of activity, a phenomenon that is larger than myself and way beyond any conceivable creation born of self-absorption, I sometimes get an edge in my voice—even when speaking to my wife. She wonders, at these times, who I am really addressing. Was I really talking to my brothers when at four years old I called myself, "Tim Jim Gray, the fastest cowboy in Cutchi Cutchi?" Shakespeare said that the entire world is a stage. Perhaps my purpose for speech sometimes is to further embed phrases and sentences into my memory. Is this really talking to myself?

How can I make the claim: I had a "selfless duty to be concerned with myself?" And how is it that this duty ended on July 18, 2005, thus ending an affliction from which I had been suffering since 1978? *You can't be a ghost, you got to be a spirit.*

My first psychiatric problem landed me at Walter Reed Army Medical Center in Washington, DC, in June of 1990. A nurse working on my ward was adamant when he spoke to me about how things were going there at WRAMC. He wanted to know the status of the *work* I was doing on my *recovery*. This theme was stressed and emphasized throughout the three months I spent on the acute ward.

The irony is that I was never tagged as being self-absorbed until after July of 2005. My impression is that people viewed me as immature, distant, and preoccupied, even masochistic—but not self-absorbed. The only exception, I must concede, took the form of my behavior when I was giddy with excitement at the prospect of being with a woman on whom I'd fixated, or one with whom I'd been obsessed. In these cases—my sister used to try to impress upon me—it was as though I were looking through glass at the female on the other side and choosing to comb my hair in my reflection afforded by the glass rather than learning anything more about my love interest. My sister would ask a question about the woman I was taken with, and my answer would be centered on me and how I felt instead of on the loved one.

These brushes with romance, however, were like little stifled gasps for oxygen. Most of the time, nearly all the time, my life was stoic and emaciated when it came to physical affection, feelings of tenderness, and intimacy. The thought of losing a friend, one who had spent *quality* time with me, shook me to the bone with dread. I lived in fear of never being able to replace the friendships I'd been able to form—with new ones. The past two years have become the first time in my life that I've been able to move on and breathe deeply the morning air. It is no coincidence that the two years began with repentance, God's forgiveness, and renewal.

Today is February 3, 2012. I've said that 2010 and 2011 were years in which I breathed deeply the "morning air." If the date in July of 2005 was such an awakening, why did it take me until the end of 2009 to emerge into that morning air? It is true that I was maturing during these four years. I had started as an eight-year-old who had repeatedly tried to emerge during my twenties, unsuccessfully. This inner child blinked in the summer sunshine, barely daring to believe that, this time, he was out for good. But it is the concept of repentance that really made the difference in my life at the end of 2009 and at the start of 2010. God changed everything.

I wrote this poem the other day:

I am resolved
I will no longer dredge the pond
Not when there is so much wildlife
And such
To be enjoyed
Here above the surface
Chirping in the trees
Or rustling through the grass
When the ecosystem
Itself
Is doing so well

Dredging
"To clean, deepen, or widen with a dredge"
Many times in the past
The process has felt good
Feeling a scab healing
And finally removed
Feeling trauma
Slowly ebbing away and out of me
Clutching trauma
Close to my chest
In times gone by
At another time
When it was difficult
To feel alive

Such an effort
It used to be
Such an effort indeed
To pry my identity out of the muck
My persona
To have it lifted clean by God
My soul
To relinquish
This death grip on control

The sun is shining
Life is sweet
There is no more need
To be contrived
Or sit upon the judgment seat
I can enjoy
With every breath
Christ's victory over death

This bittersweet sentiment with which I have been obliged to regard my own life, my own history, reminds me of what a friend of mine said to me in 2009. He said that he wouldn't trade his experience with mental illness for a million dollars, but that he also would not consent to go through it again, even if he were paid the same sum.

So my resolve to refrain from dredging the pond is a concession on my part. I shouldn't have to constantly look back into my past to come up with meaningful and satisfying evidence of what I am perceiving. In fact, should there be such a need, then my great contention that something very big is afoot and moving toward climax breaks down and disappears. Sean Connery, in the movie *The Untouchables*, advises: "Don't wait for it to happen. Don't even want it to happen. Just watch what does happen." I am therefore obliged to be watchful for what is happening now, not for what happened five years ago or ten years ago. In the October 24, 2011 issue of *Time* magazine, Hari Simran Singh Khalsa was quoted as having said,

> The exact concrete solutions may not have materialized yet, but the wonderful thing about it is we're open to change and ready for some actual paradigm shift.

My having scribbled down this quote three months ago is an example of how I am "watching" for what "does happen."

So I am pushed and pulled in opposite directions, sometimes envisioning for this book many sketches of many vignettes describing what has happened in my past, sometimes caught up with desire not to bring in past experiences at all. The vignettes seem to be desperate to find expression. Perhaps the key factor, again, is to refrain from interpreting what I am recalling, what I am sketching.

4

When my mother hears me make the statement, "My life without the grandiose stuff is a hollow shell," it does not sting her nearly as much as it did in recent years. This is largely because my life has changed so dramatically. In the past, I would keep the grandiose thoughts to myself much of the time, especially when I was interacting with my parents. When I could contain it no longer, I sometimes gushed for hours about the ways in which the grandiose scenario had developed since the last time I'd talked about it to my parents. They undoubtedly viewed these times as examples of some variation of a relapse and hoped I would get better again soon. One such time found me describing to them what sounded like a budding romance until they realized, with deflation, that I had in mind a television actress I had never met. My illness has been compared to diabetes, in that it can be treated but not cured. My mother is relieved because, while my brain does have a tendency to make loose associations, I am now enclosed in the loving arms of my wife, who loves God. My entire family, I'm sure, is similarly relieved. My father was the pastor who performed the marriage last September.

I told my wife the other day about an example that came to my mind of what would surely have been a loose association had my mind made the connection. It would have been loose for me to have linked the word she uses to sign her artwork with the proper name of a character in a movie I saw. I didn't make any such connection, but had I been without any medication in my system, I might have. What might have complicated the issue is that the word in question is emphasized in the lyrics of a song by a group whose work I consider to have many references to me and what I've done.

One classic example of what the people around me would term a loose association is what happened in the spring of 1992, during semester number eight of my time at the big state university. Amiri Baraka was making his "bombastic speech," which had begun with the man stating, and then repeatedly emphasizing, that he was about to take lozenges to treat his sore throat. My brain associated the lozenges Baraka was taking for his throat with the medication I was supposed to be taking for my mental illness, the medication I had been without for about four months. My interpretation is that Baraka may have been saying to me, "You may have to take some of your medication if you are going to be successful at what you're trying to do."

I have recently mused upon the theological question: "What is man's greatest need?" Is it to know that his sins are forgiven? Maybe it's to get to the point at which he can love God. After all, Christ says that the greatest commandment is to, "Love the Lord your God with all your heart, and with all your soul, and with all your mind." What I went through in 1990 at the age of twenty-one was spiritual turmoil involving what I could later see was my inability to accept absolution. I had a terrible time answering someone who simply asked me to state and confess my sins. I had a terrible time believing a pastor who told me that my sins were forgiven. But interwoven throughout the entire experience, interwoven throughout my entire life up to that point, was deep love for God. If I had died when I collapsed with acute heat stroke at Marine Corps Officer Candidates School, wouldn't I have died with my greatest need met—even if I had died without feeling that my sins were forgiven? Wasn't my greatest need to love God? The saddest part of the story is that, at the age of twenty-one, I couldn't remember the last time I'd said, in a prayer to God, "I love you, God." I thought at the time that saying these words had too much of a sexual connotation—which sounds pretty silly to me now. Christ didn't say, "Say these specific words in prayer." He said, "Love." I love God.

Salvation, I have heard defined as, "reconciled relationship with God." Is it a matter of the chicken or the egg? Can we truly obey the greatest commandment without Christ's work of reconciliation on the cross? Perhaps I had spent a lifetime loving God—even if I couldn't say, "I love you, God" in prayer—because I'd been exposed to the Gospel throughout that lifetime, the Gospel that declares, "Your sins are forgiven." I am blessed. My wife even said to me, "I'm blessed with your past."

When I was a child, I spent a lot of time with my three brothers and my sister. I find it curious to look back on and recall the accusation that never failed to sweep the legs out from under any one of the five of us: "You think you're cool!" Any time one sibling resorted to this icy blast and leveled it at another, the one being addressed was obliged to completely rethink his or her position, because even the remote possibility that such censure was warranted, that one might actually have been caught thinking that one was cool, was an eventuality that left one full of angst—maybe even full of the German word, *anfectung*, which has no English equivalent.

I think it's appropriate to mention a phrase, written on a scrap of paper, I came up with before beginning this book. I was trying to give myself some direction as to where I wanted to go with the book, my third book. My wife suggested that I put up a bulletin board in my office, the office that is in the apartment we just moved into at the end of March, 2012. I pinned the scrap of paper to the board. It says, "… about the truth of who I am and how little that depends on whether I am right." I watched a movie with my wife a few nights ago, and she conceded that she could readily understand why I might identify with the main character.

My uncle died on March 28. He was one of only five people to whom I sent a hardback copy of my second book. I wrote this poem to him in 2011:

> Fifteen years ago
> I left my parents' home
> When I was 27 years old
> To spend five months in yours
> To spend my weekdays alone
> Except for the little Schipperke
> And except for the times
> The regular times
> You came home for lunch
> Together we listened to the music
> That is so much a part of you
> And I drank up the logic
> From your lips
> That which I had been starving for
> We studied the book of Genesis
> Me, my aunt, and my uncle
> Together with those in your home
> Also being exposed to the Word
> Once a week
> Once a week
> Thank you for

The Arby's sandwiches
You brought home for dinner
But most of all
Thank you for the respect you have
For the opinions of another
For the faith you have in Christ
Which you so freely shared
Thank you for reading
The books I wrote
For being mentor, friend, father
As well as my uncle

My uncle was very proud of me, of all the ways I've grown over the years, whether or not I'm right. My wife and I attended a group on recovery this morning that is based on one's strengths. My uncle encouraged me to remember my strengths and not to dwell on my weaknesses. My aunt and uncle's Christmas wish for my wife and me was to remember 2 Corinthians 12:9–10 (NIV):

> But [the Lord] said to me, "My grace is sufficient for you, for my power is made perfect in weakness." Therefore I will boast all the more gladly about my weaknesses, so that Christ's power may rest on me. That is why, for Christ's sake, I delight in weaknesses, in insults, in hardships, in persecutions, in difficulties. For when I am weak, then I am strong.

The book I'm writing now is an attempt to discern what it means to be strong and what it means to be weak, what it means for my wife and me to have each other to shore up each other's weaknesses, to celebrate each other's strengths, and to glory in Christ's power.

5

I ended my second autobiographical book by maintaining that, while I had acknowledged that I was in relationship with God, I was alone on my planet. I described the people in my life as "orbiting" around me. In the middle of August, 2011, my wife asked this brain-teasing question: "When am I going to join you on my planet?" It seemed to me at the time that I had discovered another person living on my planet, but in a region I had not yet explored. My planet was her planet. It was just as much hers as mine. I finished composition of my second book within a few days of meeting her in October of 2010. I'm getting a lot of satisfaction from seeing this metaphorical construction with which I ended book two—begin to erode and fall by the wayside, as it becomes possible in my mind that there may be others living on "my" planet.

I recently finished reading the book, *The Autobiography of Medgar Evers*, by Myrlie Evers-Williams and Manning Marable. A draft of a speech Medgar Evers was to have made appears at the end of the book. One line reads as follows: "Those who have achieved a semblance of success and cry out in a great loud voice, 'Look what I have done all by myself,' are the world's biggest fools."

I ended both of the autobiographical books I wrote with the words "*Soli Deo Gloria*," which means, "To God alone be the glory." But the four-year-old who went around saying, "I'm Tim Jim Gray, the fastest cowboy in Cutchi Cutchi," has matured into a man with a distinct tendency to allow himself to think: "If one can back it up, it ain't bragging." The purpose I have been able to identify—that which ties my life together and gives it unity and integrity—is that there was a reason God called me to take on the tremendous challenge I faced in my early twenties. What I continue to suspect is that many people will eventually be interested in reading about what happened to me and why. I sense that people will become very familiar with the events of my life and that, by writing about this subject matter, I have the privilege and opportunity to weave into the writing—in context—my witness to the love I've experienced from Christ Jesus, even though I haven't actually seen Christ in a physical, biological way.

So I find it rather fatiguing and annoying when people try to make the argument to me: "But you have no evidence for the claims you make. You are just so wrapped up in yourself that you have concocted this story to make yourself feel important." As I heard in the movie, *Rob Roy*, honor is something that no one can give to a man and that no one can take from a man. It's the "gift a man gives to himself." It is my prerogative to give to myself an unusually noble and heroic version of my time so far on this earth. No one is going to take this gift from me.

Goethe said, "If you would create something, you must be something." I must *be* the person I firmly believe God has crafted with tender, loving hands. My improving posture is a concrete way that this struggle is taking shape in my life. I attended a book club for a while at which a woman shared what she had read somewhere. The idea was to imagine all of one's troubles gone and then picture waking up the following morning. What would come first that morning? The challenge was to *be* the untroubled person, that in so doing, one would have a hand in the creation of a better future.

At the age of nine and throughout my adolescence, I had to believe that I *was* the person I thought I was, even if this knowledge was deep in my subconscious. It required faith. What resulted, what developed, what survived, finally found an arena in which to operate—when I enrolled at the big state university at the age of eighteen. Five years later, the challenge was to *be* the person I had been during those five years, even if the memory was buried deep in my subconscious.

I took action during the five years. The predominant calling I felt from God after it was over was to write about what had taken place. I don't mean to say my life was devoid of any action afterward, that it was lacking action for the next two decades, but I am saying that I sense a different calling now. What I've written so far in this book has been a wrestling process with one overriding purpose: to discern what should come next in my life.

Today is June 13, 2012. Back in April, my father made a point while leading a Bible study, that the Greek word *stigma* is translated in the NIV Bible as "marks" in the following verse: "Finally, let no one cause me trouble, for I bear on my body the marks of Jesus" (Galatians 6:17, NIV). Perhaps my father was subconsciously bringing to the front of his mind the idea that I have had to deal, throughout my adult life, with the stigma associated with mental illness.

Today is September 10, 2012. What in the world happened during this past summer? I have been away from this computer. The cyclone came by and whisked me off to the land of Oz. I am convinced that my home, where I lived with my wife, was under satanic oppression for the entire month of July. I believe that the oppression ended when my wife sprinkled holy water onto the walls and blessed our home in the name of the Father, the Son, and the Holy Spirit.

Throughout the entire month of July, my voice had an edge to it when I spoke to my wife. I raised my voice in anger almost constantly throughout the month. I told her, at the end of July, that we had, in spite of the conflict, covered much more ground in our conversations, in our arguments, and disagreements than we had in the previous eighteen months of our relationship. I reminded her that there had been times during the first eighteen months when I had repeated the same story from my past several times, as if I didn't remember—or wasn't aware—that she had already heard the story. July was different.

I titrated off the last of my antipsychotic medication over three weeks, three weeks that ended in early July. I had been on three heavy-duty psych meds for years and years. The last one went and took with it an undergirding that my mind needed to function. I began to decompensate. I gradually began to exhibit symptoms that I hadn't suffered from in any significant way since 1996, the year of my last psychiatric hospitalization. That was sixteen years ago!

I was hospitalized again on August 9, 2012. I was in the psychiatric ward for exactly three weeks. But the strange thing is that what my wife had done with the holy water, which simply means water that has been blessed, ended what I describe as the "oppression" plaguing our home. That happened on the last day of July. I tried to treat my wife better in August than I had in July. I tried to gather my wits about me and avoid hospitalization. But the paranoia I experienced was only getting worse.

6

What in the world happened during the summer of 2012? Perhaps one should start, when seeking an explanation, with the question I just wrote. The Christian faces three enemies at all times here on this earth: Satan, the world, and his own sinful nature. July and the satanic oppression accompanying it came and went. August was about the world. I came out of the local library on August 6, 2012, having just spent an hour or so on the secure library computer. I don't think I'm being paranoid when I write that, while I was typing in my password, not one but two different agents sat down next to me with the intention of observing my hands on the keyboard as I was typing in this password. After the first time, I promptly changed my password, which apparently and immediately triggered another agent to sit in the same place as the first and attempt, this time with little success—I think—to once again "steal" my password.

I walked out of the library and told my waiting wife what I thought had just transpired, and she seemed unnaturally agitated and unnerved to hear the news that I had changed my password. After she suggested that I leave my briefcase with her as I go, alone, into the grocery store, my mind suffered something of a hemorrhage. Was my marriage to this woman nothing more than her assignment, her attempt to gain intelligence for my nemesis? Was she nothing more than a double agent?

When I was hospitalized three days after having this *realization* outside the library, I was sent to a large facility about three hours from my home. Without any medication in my system—and I had been without medication for just over a month at this point—I continued to deteriorate and decompensate. Before leaving my home city, I had told a bizarre, unbelievable tale to an admitting doctor in the emergency room, and he had petitioned that I be *involuntarily committed* to a psychiatric ward. I had been deemed a danger to myself, perhaps even a danger to others, and I left for the larger city, three hours away, in handcuffs and in the back of a police car.

After one hour on the road, I suddenly broke into song. I sang—only one time through—the refrain from the song by Twisted Sister: "We're not gonna take it. No! We're not gonna take it. We're not gonna take it—anymore!" The two policemen in the front seat chuckled to themselves, and we exchanged a bit of conversation. I had been quite sedate up to that point. Two hours into the trip, I once again sang the refrain from a song I really loved, a children's song by Michael Card: "The Word is so near to your heart and your tongue, with the one you confess and acknowledge the Son, with the other believe and are justified—And find life in knowing it was for you He died." This once again triggered a few remarks from the stalwart cops in the front seat. Three hours into the trip, just before reaching our destination, I got a bit more unruly and began singing again, and again, and again, the refrain from the song by Peter, Paul, and Mary: "Puff, the magic dragon, lived by the sea, and frolicked in the autumn mist in a land called Honnely." I was getting emotional as I was singing this last selection, and I had trouble keeping myself from slipping into different octaves and different keys. The driver of a pickup, alongside the police car with the singing, cuffed occupant, yelled out that the song was from 1969, which didn't come as any surprise to me since I believed that my beloved country had undergone a siege from 1963 to 1968, that the children's song about a dragon was full of analogous meaning. Instead of "autumn mist"; however, I was singing the words, "open air," because I had only been familiar with the song for less than twenty-four hours, and I didn't have even the refrain memorized.

Today is October 18, 2012. I have been home from the psych ward since August 29 and am living with my parents. I find myself going through the stages of grief that come with a divorce. The process of dividing up possessions, etc., has been expedited and moved along by my wife, beginning before the word *divorce* was mentioned by either party. I must admit that I was the first to mention the word when I wrote a letter to her from the psych ward. The legal jargon, "the objects of matrimony have been destroyed," seem to me to take on new meaning in this case because of what I suspect about my wife, that her objectives were not honorable.

I am responsible for having decided to go without my medication for over a month, and I acknowledge that I have a thought and mood disorder that, without the medication as treatment, leaves me careening toward relapse and, ultimately, psychosis. What I do not acknowledge is that all of the associations I have made in the past, the associations that sound crazy to almost everyone, are without the merit of credulity when put into proper context and given a fair hearing. Yes, the story sounds bizarre and unbelievable, but sometimes the truth is just that.

My first two books were all about providing an exposition of what happened to me and why. What I am attempting to do with this book is to report the *consequences* of what I believe has happened—the consequences for everyone. What I believe about my wife falls into this category. I think that some exposition is appropriate for this book. Previously, I have stated that I should not try to interpret what I am writing about. This is because the big leap for me is to acknowledge that "my world" is the same one on which others are walking. I am NOT alone on my planet. Admitting that is, in itself, the next big step for me.

7

To carry the metaphor further, those I felt were "orbiting around me" while I was supposedly alone on my planet needed to have the action and events transpiring on my planet interpreted for them. They were, by definition, aliens. The realization I have come to is that what goes on beyond the wall, the wall in front of me, the wall hiding what I can't be sure of, affects me directly and indirectly. I am on the same planet as the person behind the wall in front of me. Indeed, it is the definition of *intelligence* to be able to, with varying degrees of success, imagine what is going on behind a wall, what is concealed from one's actual, physical vision.

What I have become more and more conscious of, what I have gone through degrees of awakening to, is that there is a world beyond the wall in front of me and that it is very real. My impressions now of my ex-wife, what flits about in my memory when I think of her, is that she may be the first person to have occupied positions both on my side of the wall and on the other side of the wall in front of me. I have no contact with her. The divorce was final on December 4. Today is January 9, 2013.

I must confess that I am now operating, perhaps more so than at any other time in my life, now existing on both sides of the wall. I feel I have a grandiose life that I am engaged in. I also feel as though I have a three-dimensional life. As I've hinted at throughout this book, what God did through me in my early twenties is real for me and has been, especially since July 18, 2005, but now the cork is really off the bottle! When I was in the psychiatric ward last August, I spent much of my free time hovering around the central desk, trying to be of help here and there to the staff. Patients even began to assume that I *was* staff, perhaps some kind of lawyer. Once, someone near the desk asked someone else, "Is it your birthday?" I stated emphatically, to no one in particular and so that all nearby could hear, "No, it's mine."

I'm celebrating my "birthday," which was on August 12, 2012, by emphasizing to myself that I am now fully awake, even more so than when the light switched on that day: July 18, 2005. I now realize that I can take nothing for granted when it comes to how grandiose my situation is. It now seems entirely possible that wiretaps are in place at sites I frequent most, that this may have been the case for quite some time.

What leads me to suspect that this outrageous thing is true is that I sent my first autobiographical book by e-mail in the spring of 2006 to what seems now like a scam in New York City, a literary agency catering to unpublishable writers. It seems to me now that it is quite likely that my writing reached, eventually, the hand of my nemesis, the man about whom I have been quite nebulous so far in this current manuscript, my third book. After my "birthday" last August, I suggested to one of the workers in the ward that my 2006 "blunder" may have been an act of leadership, that I may have been looking ahead and thinking that the legal principle of discovery would be best served if the opposition had the relevant material in hand. Maybe I thought that ambushing my nemesis all at once with everything would ultimately weaken the case.

In any event, the upshot is that I do not know who is listening, should there be wiretaps in place at places I frequent most. In fact, I suspect that any words I create— any that are digitalized by computer—may also be open for scrutiny by the "bad guys," which means that these very words I am writing right at this instant may be under review. If that is the case, then IN YOUR FACE if you are my enemy. It is also quite possible that the "good guys" are also listening and reading every word I utter or tap into the keyboard.

The reason I suspect that the good guys are definitely listening is what transpired at the end of January, 2011. That's when the relationship with my ex-wife began. I heard, while on three different doses of heavy-duty antipsychotic medication, a little ditty coming from somewhere in my apartment. The words were such as to imply that "someone" did not want me to dive in to a relationship with the woman who is now my ex-wife. I don't think the ditty was a hallucination. Similarly, when my parents looked up the New York City scam on the Internet, looking to keep me from sending my first book and surrendering myself to a bad contract, the good guys may have been working overtime to try to keep me from making the blunder by making sure that many warnings came under the purview of my parents, Web sites that warned of the agency being a scam.

But because I must remain an isolated variable, I couldn't be contacted directly and kept from making either mistake: starting with my ex-wife or sending the manuscript. As I've said, however, I now believe that I may know someone who occupies a space on the other side of the wall, someone I suspect may know my nemesis very well. The closest I've come in the past to knowing someone on the other side of the wall is having had contact with my nemesis himself and the two people I consider to be his cohorts.

One of the reasons, I think, *The Informant* made it all the way to being made into a movie was that the corporate spy in the true story, the man who experiences manic-depressive or bipolar symptoms, gushes at one point to the opposing team of lawyers. He gives them everything they need to help them make their case. The most insidious element of this entire turn of events for me is that I fully realized what I'd done in 2012, but the act had occurred in 2006. No one could alert me to the fact, starting in 2006, that I needed to start keeping my mouth shut, to watch what I put onto my computer screen, etc. The best that could be done was to put the idea into the form of a movie and hope that I would get the message.

The reason, of course, that wiretaps might be justified for little ole me is that I implicated my nemesis and his cohorts, in my first book, the one I e-mailed to the literary agency, as having done something quite dastardly, something that had national security issues at stake. I didn't name names, but I can't rule out the possibility that some unscrupulous person thought it advantageous to figure out the identity of the man in question, my nemesis, and get the book to him.

8

Now the cork is really off the bottle. I believe that the movie, *Our Idiot Brother*, about a lovable and highly principled man who can't keep his mouth shut, was inspired by my story. I believe that a case has been building against my nemesis and his cohorts since 1992, after I had made some identifications in a secure, psych ward setting, but that, once those identified knew that they were being hunted, which happened in the spring of 2006 when I sent my book to the scam, the good guys lost the advantage of their quarry being oblivious to what was happening.

The importance of these identifications, as I have repeatedly tried to explain to my father, is that they put nearly everyone on the same side of the line. No one, ultimately, is going to want to be associated, in the end, with my nemesis and his cohorts. I have sought to mobilize the masses and, even more importantly, to *unify* the masses. Most of the time, these days, I feel quite convinced that I have helped to do just that, all by the grace of God. The celebrative and "anthemic" album called *Battle Born*, recently produced in 2012 by the band called The Killers, I believe, is all about me getting back on my feet and not surrendering, even though I have been knocked down, with my heart broken after realizing that my ex-wife was working for the enemy.

My penchant for blabbing and not keeping my mouth shut started back in 1990, before I had made the necessary identifications, while I was still working hard to understand the mission in front of me. I was being discharged from the military due to the fact that I was no longer medically qualified to become a Marine Corps officer, because I had come down with a mental illness at Officer Candidates School in Quantico, Virginia. I believe that the "good guys," those working in a counterrevolutionary effort to overthrow those who came to power during the revolution that occurred from 1963 to 1968, found it rather annoying that I "blabbed" about my case to my state representative by writing him a letter, which stated that my situation was anomalous and needed to be expedited, that I wanted to be home by Christmas. I was told that I was the first person in the history of the Marine Corps to have been switched from ACDUTRA, my status at OCS, to active duty. This switch was necessary because I needed ongoing care in the psych ward at Walter Reed Army Medical Center after being sent there from Quantico in June of 1990. I was home by Christmas, but there was probably a lot of light shed on my predicament, revealing to lots of unknown entities the peculiar nature of my lot in life, the mission I was faithfully pursuing.

So I awoke on July 18, 2005 to the realization that my grandiose beliefs were not, for the most part, delusional. On November 16, 2009 I believe I was vindicated when I understood for the first time that there had been consequences resulting from my behavior. After all, I read once that "what humans regard as real has real consequences." But I did not awake fully to the realization that the bad guys have been alerted to my existence and are forming their case for the defense until just last August, that their efforts have been helped along the way by my being oblivious to what I'd done in 2006.

But the question is, was I truly oblivious, or was I thinking of the big picture? The Killers sing in the song, "The Rising Tide," "Can you tell me though, was I deceived or in denial?" Did I know full well, all along, that my ex-wife might have been a double agent? Maybe what the movie, *Our Idiot Brother*, praises about the hero, played by Paul Rudd—his quixotic tendency to expect the best from people despite the fact that Rudd's character is almost constantly confronted with people *not* responding this way, perhaps this fictional characterization was inspired by me and my naive and innocent hope that my ex-wife would live up to what I was expecting from her. The quote from the movie goes like this: "I live my life a certain way—that if you put your trust out there, really give people the benefit of the doubt and see their best intentions, they are going to want to live up to it. It doesn't always work out—clearly—but more often than not, I think that if you do this, people will rise to the occasion."

In the movie, *Michael Clayton*, which came out a couple years after my 2006 blunder, a children's book is described whose title and content was created just for the movie. Clayton's son desperately wants his father to read the book. The son states that, in the book, "there are no borders, or landmarks, or anything…and nobody has any alliances. You can't even say who you are because, you don't know, maybe the person you're talking to—maybe they're like your mortal enemy in the wars, so it's just completely like everybody for themselves." Clayton responds, "Sounds familiar." Clayton's jaded and worn-down apathy is really the subject of the movie. The movie is a call to arms, a "summons to conquest," as it is put in the fictional children's book. And I can't help but believe that what inspired the writer/director, Tony Gilroy, to create the movie is the soup I immediately created in the spring of 2006 when I seemingly threw everything into chaos by serving up the sensitive information in my first book to my nemesis, as though to give him a better chance of keeping up the pace.

9

The rather stupendous conclusion I reached at the end of the previous chapter leaves me feeling quite odd and even a bit queasy in the stomach as I begin this one. I have made a decision to go without caffeine as I tackle life's challenges in the future. Large doses of caffeine enhanced the formation of loose associations in my mind over the last eight months or so. I admit that what ties together the elements of my grandiose scenario often involves associations that are "loose." These associations seem worse, or even more loose, when I try to describe the scenario by mentioning only two or three items from a list that probably runs into the hundreds by now, hundreds of points I could make in an attempt to convince my listener that my place on the earth is grandiose in nature.

Just one example of what I mean concerns one of the four bands I maintain make many references to me and my work—and my mistakes!—in the many albums they have released over the past decade or so. One of the bands is called Wilco and on their album called *The Whole Love*, there is a song that says, "But I still say we're too old for clichés." My first book, in its present, unpublished state anyway, contains lots and lots of clichés.

This is the same book that, in all likelihood, I sent to my nemesis in the spring of 2006 when I made my big blunder. This reference to clichés is not, of course, convincing if taken alone. One of the other bands is called Finger Eleven, and they have a song on an album called, "Them vs. You vs. Me," that employs the word *was* and the word *were*. What I find unusual and intriguing is that, within one song, the booklet that contains the song's lyrics shows both the correct and the incorrect use of the words. This is what I mean: "If one *were* to use the word correctly…" is the correct way to say it. "If one *was* to use the word…" is not correct. Finger Eleven's written lyrics break the rule and adhere to the rule in the same song! In my first book, again in its present form, I made the mistake again and again.

Recently, I heard Norm DeLisle speak on leadership, and he defined the word *strategy* as a "way to deal with scarce resources and an uncertain future." What goes along with having the big picture in mind is that it is difficult to trust one perspective over another as to how the world is defined and represented in one's mind. I'm thinking specifically about myself at the age of six when I heard from another boy in the neighborhood that JFK had been killed by a Marine. The impression I formed at that time was more sustainable in my mind than, for example, later news that the assassination had been carried out by Lee Harvey Oswald. I believe that I formed a strategy for doing what I could to help bring about justice, a strategy that involved trying to become an officer in the Marine Corps. Indeed, as a sophomore at my big state university, I signed on the line committing myself to at least four years as an officer or, if unsuccessful at becoming an officer, at least two years as an enlisted man. Norm DeLisle also stated that "planning" is often more difficult than problem solving because one must conceive of an endpoint, regardless of whether it seems possible.

One reason I am referring to the time span of 1963 to 1968 in America as one in which a "revolution" occurred is that I don't trust other definitions of the time in question. My very astute older sister once explained to me what the point of Marine Corps Officer Candidates School was: "to instill in the initiate trust in his superior officers." If one goes with all the crazy suppositions I make, then it was ultimately my superiors in the counterrevolution who played that little ditty in my apartment, the one that seemed to be warning me not to become involved with the woman who is now my ex-wife.

I remember one line from the "ditty" in particular: "You treat me like I've got green polka dots." The little song wasn't explicitly warning me away from my ex-wife. It was marveling at how stubborn and close-minded I was being when I considered the prospect of meeting and perhaps falling in love with my long-time obsession, a beautiful movie star. I don't think I considered the ditty a hallucination. I was on three heavy-duty dosages of three different antipsychotics at the time. I think I failed to trust my superior "officers" in this case. I had been speaking to my ex-wife on the phone for hours at a time for two weeks when I heard the little song. I had been considering the prospect of falling once more for the movie star for about seven weeks when I heard the little song. The "walls" that Finger Eleven sings about in their album called *Life Turns Electric* had been gradually breaking down under what I must say was also some pretty serious criticism of me and how I had handled the romance with the movie star up to that point. It was as though I chose my ex-wife over the movie star, or over the prospect of meeting her. I don't claim that I have ever been in relationship with the movie star, though I admit that I used to make that claim, but I do maintain that we have been involved in a "romance." The classic definition of romance always includes absence. The ending, "and they lived happily ever after," is never what the story is about. I also freely admit that I used to be obsessed with the movie star, whom I will call WR. I have never met her. I have never received mail from her or been contacted by her.

10

Now the cork is really off the bottle. I feel like I've caught up, in my conscious mind, to what I now face. I'm learning these days—today is March 27, 2013—just how precarious my hold is on my sanity. But I am back to being heavily medicated, and I feel that the future is simply going to be challenging. What's so bad about that? At Marine Corps OCS, the commanding officer addressed us in an auditorium. Among his last exhortations were the words, "And make no mistake—you will be challenged!"

In a song called "Whole Love" from the album called *The Whole Love*, Wilco repeats three times the words, "And I know that I won't be the last/ Cold captain tied to the mast." I see this as a reference to my leadership position. The album came out in 2011, when I was still tied to my ex-wife. What I wonder is whether the line could be referring to the idea that the musicians making up the four bands I cite as especially significant may have felt that they would have to carry me kicking and screaming into consciousness, the consciousness that I made the wrong choice as to which woman I was going to pursue and woo. They might have to "tie me to the mast" whether I liked it or not. But the strange thing is that I came to the realization about my ex-wife being a double agent *before* I purchased *The Whole Love*, before I purchased the album by The Killers called *Battle Born*. The album by The Killers came out on September 17, 2012, about five weeks after I was admitted to the psych ward after decompensating last summer. I can't help but believe that the production and distribution of the finished album was accelerated, that the album has songs with references to my summer of 2012, even references to my psych ward stay, at least the very beginning of it.

I refer often to the month of January, 2011 because it was so pivotal. During the month, I essentially chose to pursue my ex-wife instead of my longtime love interest, the movie star—WR. I finished a three-thousand-word letter to my little brother in January of 2011, lamenting the fact that Finger Eleven's album, *Life Turns Electric*, had opened old wounds in me, that I was struggling to maintain the very walls the band sings about in their music. It had been about two years since I'd sent a letter to WR's fan mail address. I'd finished my second book during the two years, a book which wrestles with how I handled the "romance." In the letter to my brother, I reach a climax by saying, "But WR never asked to become my false god."

I believe it is essential for me to make clear that, while WR never contacted me directly, I can afford to gather that she has been interested, at least at times, in me for romance. What convinces me of this is the character of the lyrics sung by the four bands. To put it in simple, grade school terms, when a preteen is interested in one of his or her classmates, that preteen does not address the object of the affection directly. Some helpful peer walks up to the loved one and states, "So and so *likes* you." To put it once again in simple terms, I feel that the groups Finger Eleven, Five for Fighting, and Wilco have generally been on the side of WR when they assess the situation and my behavior. The Killers have seemed to be on my side of the conflict. They have seemed to empathize with me and feel for the way I might have internalized the criticism from the other three bands.

All four of the bands have functioned as a grade school peer whispering to me, "WR likes you." What has accompanied the whisper differs depending on which side one wishes to join. My behavior has been reprehensible at times. Wilco sings a song from a 2001 album called *Yankee Hotel Foxtrot*—it's titled, "I am trying to break your heart." My behavior has seemingly gotten worse, not better, as each castigating album is produced. Wilco's 2009 album features these lyrics: "Deeper down/ He felt the insult of a kiss."

The idea seems to be that WR is going to care for me regardless of how badly I have treated her. The band seems to be saying, especially in 2011, when they came out with *The Whole Love*, that it would be such a wondrous, remarkable thing if I would simply open my mind.

I wrote my second book in an effort to process how badly I had botched the romance with WR. I was somewhat cavalier at first until I discovered a song by Five for Fighting called, "Story of Your Life," from the album called *Slice*, which includes these lines, describing what happened what "he" did to a young actor: "He left her broken like you figured, like you knew he would /She shut her heart after his ring rang off the door." I spent the rest of the time composing the book in a spirit of repentance and finished it with an open apology. I had sent a ring along with a letter to WR in the summer of 2006. So when I compounded my mistakes by choosing my ex-wife over WR in January of 2011, WR presumably had to, if she were to hold out hope of being with me, simply wait for me to come to my senses, for my subconscious to assert itself, for me to be free again, which happened on December 4, 2012—when my divorce was final.

11

During the "pivotal" month of January, 2011, I had been listening to Finger Eleven's album called *Life Turns Electric*. From the moment I heard the songs—and I feel they all have reference to my story—to the moment I heard the little ditty coming from somewhere in my apartment, amounted to seven weeks of circumspection on my part. However, I "chose" to pursue my ex-wife and continue treating WR as though she had green polka dots. In fact, shortly after hearing the ditty, I dropped WR from my conscious mind.

Today is April 8, 2013. I am drinking caffeine again, but I am trying to cut back on the amount. I have stated previously that I was vindicated on November 16, 2009, after hearing on a Five for Fighting album about how badly I had treated WR. "She shut her heart after his ring rang off the door." I had always expected vindication to be a welcome, positive thing. But the consequences I heard about that day carried forward in me the process of repentance, which had begun earlier in the year. Vindication brought with it some serious pain. But it came exactly when I had always predicted it would come—the day after my forty-first birthday. I was now absolutely convinced that my grandiose story was true.

My second book is about why I felt compelled to write over one hundred long letters to WR's fan mail address—from the start of 2006 to the beginning of 2008—and yet seemed to be throwing up a wall between us with the attempt. In *Life Turns Electric*, Finger Eleven sings: "There's so much I haven't said." Despite the volume of my writing, I was withholding much of my true self. I was confused.

Today is May 2, 2013. I am committed once again to remaining free of caffeine. It has been about a week and a half since I have had any. Without caffeine, it is more likely for me to have an occasional doubt or two here and there as to whether my whole delusional scenario is a series of loose associations, connected by key suppositions. But even if these doubts are founded in fact, I believe my present calling in life is to write about what is going through my mind. Along with the volunteer work I do concerning peers helping peers stay out of the psychiatric ward, the writing I am able to squeeze out of my pressured, stressed psyche is my contribution to society, my attempt to give back to a nation that has given me so much, that has had in place a system that supports people like me with a small subsistence income.

And if the converse is true, if I am essentially right about my "crazy" suppositions and admittedly loose associations, then part of my contribution to society is the act of leadership, the one that puts me in the middle of a true reality, a reality to which almost no one around me subscribes.

In May of 1991, my work for a temporary agency in New York City was affected dramatically by my unusual mindset. Whether or not I'm right about the mindset really doesn't affect the fact that my work was affected to the detriment of my being able to remain employed. I had taken a mundane filing job and kept leaving my worksite to make notes on something I wanted to write.

The short chapters making up this book are emerging out of a maelstrom of pressure that results from my belief that I'm right about most of what the chapters describe. I believe that my anomalous writing features original composition that should remain, essentially, unedited, that this authenticity is part of its value. Perhaps the only addition to these chapters should be a few footnotes to clarify meaning and update significance.

To begin this book, I stated that I was trying to discern what should come next with my life, that the book is something of a transitional one. One of the biggest ways I have grown as a person since finishing my second book is by falling from what was a proud perch, one that somehow envisioned myself as destined to be free from divorce, one that puffed me up for being chaste. This pride came on top of a lot of self-aggrandizement I had been engaging in since 2005, when I "awoke" on July 18. Prior to this 2005 date, I had been in remission for eight years, which I now refer to as re-mission.

Wilco sings a line from a song called, "Solitaire": "I was wrong to believe in me only." My one hundred letters were extremely self-absorbed. I think I was lucky to get from WR in a 2007 magazine interview what I interpret as a hint that she might be interested in me. She was being interviewed at a bookstore, and the interviewer reported that WR purchased an "episodic memoir." I had sent her at the start of 2006 a copy of my first book, which is an episodic memoir.

My one hundred letters kept spinning layer after layer and tier after tier of self-absorption, but there was no check on the two-year attempt to be romantic, no way for me to gauge how my words were being received, so I just kept going and going, making one presumption after another. Then when the 2007 interview proclaimed WR as unattached and I saw that she was, "wonder of wonders," herself and not the person I had been creating in my self-absorption, I worked myself into righteous indignation and sent her a "sledgehammer farewell poem." Since much of this one-way correspondence I had been sending was digitalized and created with a word processor, and since much of it occurred after my 2006 blunder, my words had been, I believe, broadcast to many people.

12

My mind, over the past year or so, has been open to some pretty outlandish loose associations, ones that stretch credulity to the limit of my astonished audience of people who strive to reign my thoughts into what can be contained within my three-dimensional world without being affected by what I envision beyond the wall in front of me, the sequestered area my intellect is always straining to define. But I have come to the conclusion that I have outdone myself for the last year when it comes to one loose association in particular. I very recently read the words of WR when she was being interviewed in a major magazine, and I can no longer subscribe to my preposterous belief. I believe she contradicted it. This situation, of course, hits me hard, and I am shaken when it comes to all the other loose associations I have made in the past. The bottom line, however, is that my thoughts regarding WR do not depend on the rejected loose association being true, and the thoughts I have regarding my grandiose place on this earth do not depend on WR being interested in me romantically.

I must admit, however, that I am "absolutely captivated" by a song by Finger Eleven called "Ordinary Life." It makes me feel very good to suspect that there are people out there rooting for me to get together with WR. The hundreds and hundreds of little coincidences and references that make up my grandiose scenario I actively strove to relegate to the back of my mind from 1997 to 2005. Since 2005 the number has grown exponentially. The song goes, "I'm just singing my ordinary life, I just wish the world would sing with me sometimes."

It has recently occurred to me that the three thugs I identified in 1992 in a secure psych ward setting as having perpetrated a very heinous deed are miserable because their deeds have been exposed. I suspected that they were miserable when I was writing my second book, but with this third book, I am taking the realization one step further as I realize that it doesn't even matter anymore if the thugs are ever prosecuted for their crimes, or executed. Their lives have been over for years. Also in my second book, I make allowance for the three of them reaching the point at which they repent and seek forgiveness from God. But again, the actual legal prosecution really isn't even necessary. My 2006 blunder may have saved them from eventual execution by giving them a chance to seek sanctuary, etc., but they are living in a prison with no walls. This is what I believe is going on behind the wall in front of me.

The song by Finger Eleven called "Don't Look Down" illustrates what I am saying. The song goes, "Cause it's only a matter of time before you hit the ground /But until you fall, you're gonna have to live this out." That song came out at the end of 2010, and along with one other song on that album is entirely different in character from the rest, the other eight songs, which are upbeat and full of references to, not my miserable nemesis, but to the romance between WR and me. The eight songs are encouraging, despite their sometimes-critical and upbraiding nature. Their clear aim is to bring WR and me together.

When I ignored the little ditty I heard in my apartment in January of 2011, it was not because I felt that I was hallucinating or that I was questioning my sanity. It was because I *still* had not gotten to the point at which I trusted my superior officers in the counterrevolution. It frightened me that they would try to take such an overt hand in affecting the way my life was to play out.

The other reason I chose my ex-wife over WR was that I had understood my ex-wife to have made a public profession of Christian faith—a profession I had not witnessed myself. To my knowledge at the time of this writing, WR is not Christian, so I pretty much loaded everything onto this one extremely important point. It didn't matter to me if I was going to be reviled by the world for abandoning a woman who had seemingly invested so much contemplation time mulling over the idea of being with me eventually. I stated in my second book, which was finished in the fall of 2010, a few months before this momentous decision of mine, that I had been hoping WR would convert to Christianity.

I now realize, of course, that my decision was wrong, that it was a disastrous one. The lingering suspicions I had from the very beginning of my relationship with my ex-wife that she might be functioning as a double agent failed to keep me from plunging headlong into the abyss. The movie I cited earlier called *Our Idiot Brother* seems to put a positive spin, however, on the decision I made with the line that goes, "No one loves anything as unconditionally as Ned loves!" The Ned character was always expecting the best from people.

I prefer to cast the decision in the light of the Bible verse from Romans 8:28 (NIV): "And we know that in all things God works for the good of those who love him, who have been called according to his purpose." God can work even through my failings, and I prefer to believe that WR is one of those who have been "called according to his purpose."

13

I have concluded that there is no romance going on between me and WR, despite the previous indications that people seemed to be rooting for it or encouraging it. With my superfluous time for wistful recollection, I muse upon the possibility that the 2011 conclusion I made to my brother in a letter, that WR "never asked to become my false god," may strike even closer to the heart of the matter than I have considered before. This summary phrase now seems in my mind to be defining when it comes to how I characterized WR. After all, she has always resided only on the other side of the wall. For me to presume that she "simply" had to "wait" for me to come to my senses and realize that I had married a double agent, realize it in my conscious mind, seems now to be presuming too much. It surprises me to imagine that the counterrevolutionary forces could be so out of touch with the reality of the situation, how they could be so off base with their reproach, "You treat me like I've got green polka dots," but perhaps WR may have been more open to true romance with me at the time when I heard the little ditty in my apartment, January 2011. The band Five for Fighting seemed to have slammed the door shut with their November 2009 line: "She shut her heart after his ring rang off the door." The 2012 line from the Killers, "Be still, and go on to bed—nobody knows what lies ahead," is perhaps the most accurate word I can take with me into the future, a future that seems suddenly to be so mired in the 3-D world.

The concept of a 3-D world is addressed in one of my favorite books, a mid twentieth century novel by Evelyn Waugh called *Brideshead Revisited*:

> "I have left behind illusion," I said to myself. "Henceforth I live in a world of three dimensions— with the aid of my five senses."
>
> I have since learned that there is no such world; but then, as the car turned out of sight of the house, I thought it took no finding, but lay all about me at the end of the avenue.

There is a difference, one might argue, between illusion and delusion. I would counter that there is also a difference between illusion and theory, but either distraction fails to understand the one core truth: there is no such thing as a world that is only 3-D.

I find myself once again, as was the case with my previous books, in opposition to my reader. I suggested that the audience for those books was basically myself, and I asked, in this book, "How can I be in opposition to my reader if that reader is myself? Welcome to my world." The struggle to affirm for myself the legitimacy of my writing remains a challenge. My little brother wants me to write a historical novel about our grandfather, who died late in the year 1964, before either of us was born. I found myself saying at a recent family gathering that I might make the attempt after this book, my third, was finished. I think I said this mainly seeking approval, not because it falls into line with my plans. My brother says that he would write the book himself, but he does not have the time. I predict that, if I made the proposed book my fourth, I would be too carried away in my imagination to do the story justice. I have to repeat to myself: there is absolutely nothing wrong with writing books with the anomalous pattern that is found in book two and this book, number three, and there is nothing wrong with the episodic memoir I wrote first and called an autobiography. Today is June 13, 2013.

What I've written so far in this chapter, as I look it over, seems to be analogous to a woodsman fending off wolves. I began this third book with the intention of not mentioning WR. As I read over the initial chapters, I am struck with how shallow my descriptions were of my ex-wife. In January of 2011, I remember the thought occurring to me: Maybe I should steer clear of both these women. The month opened when I saw a movie at the cinema on January 2 called *How Do You Know?* At that point, I had been ruminating over the songs I'd been hearing on *Life Turns Electric* for about a month. I met my ex-wife about two and half months before going to the January 2 movie. I have notations in my little scheduling booklet noting two occasions in which I wept alone in my apartment: January 3 and January 12. As if I were not confused enough already, January 13 brought with it a rare and intriguing sight outside my sliding glass door. Two cars, parked side by side, had left two parking spaces in such a way that their tires had left imprinted in the pristine snow two shapes that formed hearts, exactly the same size. There were no stray tire marks to besmirch the mesmerizing effect. I had no idea what to make of the strange sight. On January 15 I told my mother that the album by Wilco I had purchased, the one with a picture of a camel on it, seemed to me to be suggesting that I would "break the camel's back" if I made one more rash or otherwise poor judgment error when it came to romance with WR. The next evening, at a Bible study, I gave my phone number to my ex-wife, ostensibly to lend my tutorial support for an English class she was taking at the time. On January 17 my ex-wife called me, and we talked for hours. At the climax of our talk, I told her that I was a virgin, and she declared, "Oh, that's beautiful." On January 25 I heard the little song in my apartment with the words, "You treat me like I've got green polka dots." On January 26 I left a message on my ex-wife's machine that said something like, "I choose to remain in my little alone corner." I remember being surprised that her response did not carry with it any trace of anger. On January 29, I'm quite sure, she showed me a cartoon she'd drawn with a big draft horse yoked to a little show pony and a caption that read, "I think it's time to rethink this partnership." I was hooked.

14

I have been much more content with my 3-D world since throwing myself into an attempt to begin a drop-in center here in my small city. I was among three other people who originated the attempt. We got a two-year federal start-up grant which allowed us to hire staff and procure a site for our center. I have enjoyed having this position in the public sphere for three and a half years. I have been president of the center's board of directors for two years. The board members must all be consumers of mental health services because we are a peer-run non-profit organization. I wrote this personal story with the hope that it might be used to help acquire grant money for our center:

> As president of the board of directors for [the center], I have read that I am to seek a "symbiotic" relationship with my director, the person who actually runs the place. We have been open for two and a half years, and I can remember a time when our director praised me for speaking up and encouraging her to

not be concerned so much about whether the two receptionist level employees under her were "busy" at all times. I said that such concern was at cross purposes with what we at the center were seeking to generate when it came to the general character of the atmosphere the place is supposed to offer to those with mental illnesses.

The entry level employees, just as is the case when I myself bring in work to accomplish at the center, should feel free to take breaks and feel unsupervised so that they can be free to provide, and benefit from, peer-to-peer counseling. This is very much a "play it by ear" phenomenon and is one of the greatest strengths of [our center].

This volunteer work for the center has greatly improved my concept of my 3-D world and has helped me muster the courage to take myself off the shelf and become an activist and not just an advocate.

This may seem like a loose leap, but I am reminded of my 1992 hospitalization, the one during which I identified the three thugs as having done the heinous deed. When I state that this psych ward setting was a "secure" place for me to make the identifications, I mean that my handlers, those directing the domestic espionage I had been officially engaged in from 1987 to 1992, could make direct contact with me, and such contact could later be dismissed as simply something I hallucinated on the television screen. This made me an "isolated variable," to use a psych lab term. I would always be protected by the pervasive and comprehensive blanket of doubt—I always had with me the idea that I might just be crazy. I bring this up now because I contend that these "hallucinations" on the television screen were not hallucinations at all but rather elements I perceived with the aid of my five senses and therefore part of my 3-D world.

I saw the actual face of Jesse Jackson. I saw a videotape of JFK making a speech I had never heard before, but whenever it was impossible for me to see the actual person, an actor was employed to represent the identity. I saw actors supposed to be representing my little brother and a woman I had met during the summer of 1990. I saw an actor supposed to be representing God. When psychosis, which was inevitable because I was refusing to take antipsychotic medication, finally hit me, it was really David Copperfield, the magician, I saw on the screen and not an actor. It was really Lee Majors, the actor, I saw on the screen. I believe these two people were employed to create a videotape that would bring about psychosis while I was still safely housed in a psychiatric ward, where it could be dealt with appropriately. I am putting this description in the 3-D chapter because I do not think that dopamine, the neurotransmitter that bombards the nerve ending when someone is hallucinating and creates for the ill person what he processes as perceptions, perceptions that aren't really there, was firing in my case at this time. Additionally, the television in the psych ward I was on seemed to be a two-way TV, transmitting the image of myself on the couch, at the same time it was transmitting the face of Jesse Jackson to my eyes. I think this is true because Jackson seemed to be reacting to my facial expression as he was speaking. I felt my lower lip droop into a clownish face as I heard him speak, as though I was not respecting him—and he seemed to be unnerved by my racism.

One actor seemed to be representing the identity of Malcolm X. I remember this person making a forceful statement to me: "You're going back behind the curtain where you belong!" This statement has nonplussed me for years, but I think I can finally make an attempt to explain what my handlers might have meant by it. My point is that I "heard" the statement come from the television, and I saw the square-jawed actor with his "I mean business" look on his face. It was not a case, I believe, of dopamine firing in my brain to create a perception that was not really there.

15

I have an active imagination. Perhaps that is an understatement. I feel compelled to write that my conclusion from chapter 13 of this book, that there is no romance going on between WR and me, may have been an example of my speaking too soon. The website from which I drew the conclusion states clearly that it is not an official site for WR and is not affiliated with WR or WR's people. I can therefore make no sure conclusion about what WR is thinking based on hearsay. I feel weak and foolish for having done so, even for a short time. The line from Wilco comes again to mind: "I was wrong to believe in me only." Because I have such an active imagination, I simply cannot completely rule out the preposterous loose association I spoke of in chapter 12 of this book. I am not completely satisfied that it is untrue. I am clinging to a technicality when I conclude that WR has not absolutely contradicted the possibility of it being true.

When I approached the idea of romance with WR, I led with my ass. What I mean by that is that I put my worst side forward first, perhaps out of insecurity, perhaps because I was thinking that if she is interested after my worst has been put forward, she'll be completely taken with me after I come through with my best. This concept of mine, that I must exorcise the worst from within me, has roots that reach back a long time. I believe I half-convinced myself, from age ten to age twenty-three, that a lesser demon named Perfect had entered my body and that the demon was responsible for many of the times I made the wrong move, or otherwise failed to act in an admirable way. I believe my imagination created this construction in my personality. I don't believe that my body actually housed a demon for thirteen years.

There were four times, I once wrote to WR, in which I snapped to attention at the sound of the word *perfect*, once at each of the ages seventeen, eighteen, nineteen, and twenty. When I was first hospitalized in 1990, at the age of twenty-one, I writhed in four-point restraints as though a demon had control of my body. At Quantico, before being admitted to WRAMC in 1990, I was asked while being put under hypnosis: "Have you ever been an agent for a foreign government?" I replied, in a wicked, high pitched voice and with hooded eyelids: "No, no, no—I was just playing a game!" When I was twenty-three, during my 1992 hospitalization, I wrote on one of the pages of my journal, with a date and a time, these words: "The demon has leff," and then I consciously strove to complete the word—after the demon had supposedly spent his last gasp trying to keep me from writing it—"left my body." It all started when I was about ten, after I had been admonished by my mother for running around in front of the altar of an empty church. I stopped before the altar, looked up at the cross, and defiantly put the question to God: "What's wrong with running around in front of the altar?" At that moment, I must have thought to myself, with my imagination going strong, the words, "There's nothing wrong with it, Tim, you're perfect," and concluded with some misgivings that perhaps I had even heard a voice whisper the words into my ear.

The words, therefore, coming from the actor representing Malcolm X on the psych ward television, must have been, I can only conclude, humoring my little imaginative construct. The words, "You're going back behind the curtain where you belong!" must have been addressing the demon, the nasty little creep named Perfect, the one who had been responsible for my drooping lower lip, which had made Jesse Jackson momentarily uncomfortable on the television screen.

It strikes me now as rather frightening—that some might say I could title this book I'm writing now: "One man's descent into madness." Let's take stock of the situation. I have theorized that I have powerful enemies who have placed wiretaps in the places I frequent most because I am a threat to national security. I have hopes that a movie star

I have never met and never heard from harbors romantic feelings for me. I am refusing to rule out a possibility that most people would surely say is not within the realm of what is sane. I regularly take comfort from what I perceive to be references to my situation in the lyrics of four bands whose albums I have followed for years. I have just claimed that images I saw on a psych ward television that accompanied a bout of psychosis were not the product of dopamine firing abnormally in my brain.

And yet I found myself saying just the other day that I feel stronger mentally now than at any other time in my adult life. My illness, which can be described as a thought and mood disorder, hit me first when I was twenty-one years old, barely into adulthood. I feel "awake," alive, and happy. I'm not saying there aren't some shaky moments, or feelings of doubt, but my last bout of paranoia was a full five months ago. My medication, after being released from the psych ward last August, has been reduced three times. Today is June 24, 2013.

I feel like my life has been a success. My enemies threw me, as The Killers put it in the song called "Battle Born," "up against the wall," but I am not going to surrender. I am going to heed the admonition, the charge, to "get back on your feet," that I have already done so and am feeling strong and sure of myself. I have been immersed in the Word of God, which is the only way I can account for my relatively quick recovery. I believe that what I'm writing now is a "corking good read!"

16

Today is August 16, 2013. After maintaining high velocity during June, I felt it would be good to take some time off during the summer. The previous couple of chapters of this book contain a lot of inward bound torque. I think it was traumatic for me to conclude, even for a short time, that there is no romance between me and WR. I understand that I must be prepared for being disappointed, but I simply prefer to be hopeful and imaginative. If the preposterous loose association I keep referring to is actually true, then it would be impossible for WR to be open about it to the press. Once again, the term *self-reinforcing delusion* surfaces with all its ugliness.

I really am not feeling as "on the edge of my seat" as I was when I wrote the previous paragraph a few days ago. I have just come from a medication review with one of my mental health practitioners, and my medication dosages have been reduced for the fourth time during the past year. As I've written previously, my recovery has been remarkably quick this time around. Indeed, having a relapse a year ago after sixteen years without one has served to cement in my mind that I need medication for both thought and mood. There is, however, no law against being crazy. I'm keeping most of the beliefs outlined in this book to myself.

The psychiatrist I had for the sixteen years I spent without a hospitalization told me that she would not increase my medication because of something I wrote in a book. She owns a hardcover copy of my second book and thinks highly of my writing. While writing book two, I was taking a sleep aid called Ambien, which was a hypnotic. I suppose that I was in more peril at the time. What I wound up chronicling, however, was how my use of caffeine diminished into non-existence even while the sense of surety regarding my grandiose beliefs increased in incidence and degree. One reason I feel so much stronger mentally is that I am no longer taking Ambien.

There were times, during the sixteen years, when my shrink increased my medication—which can technically be termed relapses—and there were also times I requested that my meds be reduced. Usually, when I would make such a request, my shrink would tell me that she was reluctant to reduce meds while I was "delusional." If I kept my mouth shut long enough about having the "delusional" thoughts— she sometimes reduced the dosage slightly. The bottom line, as is clearly stated in my second book, is that I have been "awake" since July 18, 2005.

In the song by Wilco called, "Black Moon," there is this line: "Okay, I'm an old shoe." The last line of the song that one hears on the CD is the repetition of the words: "Are you awake now too?" It seems to me as though Wilco is saying that I made WR feel like an "old shoe." It also seems to me that Wilco, as a group, felt that there was more to wake up to than what became clear to me in 2005. What hit the front of my mind in the summer of 2012, including the preposterous loose association I have been referring to, catches me up, at least for the time being—I would think.

17

Despite the crazy suppositions and loose associations to which I currently adhere and cling, I am functioning quite well. I am getting plenty of sleep and plenty to eat. I believe I may have reached my sweet spot when it comes to medication. I think I'm on the right amount of meds to keep my thought and mood disorder in check. I have begun to blossom and feel even more fulfilled and happy since I started seeing a clinical psychologist in town for psychoanalysis—one hour per month. I trust the man. I am cooperating with the people from Community Mental Health, including the psychiatrist I see for fifteen to twenty minutes every six months or so. During those six months, I see another practitioner for a med review. As I've said, my medication has been reduced four times during the past year. I also have a CMH therapist and a case worker.

I have a fear, however, that should the news somehow get to CMH that I have grandiose beliefs, I will be pressured to take more medication, medication I do not feel I need. I have begun, nevertheless, to be more open and broaden the number of people, including the clinical psychologist, in whom I can confide about the beliefs that sound so crazy to people in general. One recent development that has hastened this process forward is my discussion with a friend of mine who has published a book on the Internet. I'm getting to the point at which my small subsistence income is becoming inadequate. The book I'm writing now, I believe, is more palatable to the public than the two books I wrote previously. If I could generate even modest income from e-publishing this book, I would solve my financial problem and also possibly emerge, to some degree, from the obscurity in which I am currently existing. Toward this end, I have felt less inclined to keep certain material secret, since it may be brought into the open anyway if the book reaches the market.

My previous experience with psychoanalysis is confined to what occurred from the summer of 1991 to the spring of 1992—the months that comprise the touchstone year I opened the chapters of this book writing about. That was also one hour per month, but I did not trust the psychiatrist I was working with. He seemed to have huge and vast ambitions for me. I later became convinced that he was the same person who actually swung the gold watch back and forth and put me under hypnosis when I was at Marine Corps Officer Candidates School in 1990. He was adamant in his desire to wrest from me some plan for how I was going to subsist financially. When I said that I wanted to write, he responded, "One lives to write, one does not write to live."

What I did not share with the man is that I had been busily engaged in domestic espionage from 1987 on and that I wasn't getting a dime in payment for my work. In the critical spring of 1992, I refused to take medication that my shrink was actually holding up to my mouth with his hand. My brother and father were in the room and were incensed with anger as they witnessed my obstinacy. During my first 1991 session with the shrink, he had pronounced this curse: "What you do over the next twelve months will have a huge impact on how you spend the rest of your life." I needed to get rid of the shrink because I needed to officially make the identifications I have been referring to throughout this book. A psych ward was the secure place to do so because any ravings about thugs perpetrating a heinous deed that changed history could then be written off as the product of a sick mind that needed medication to return to normal. The identifications I made on paper in the psych ward I knew were being tossed into a waste basket by a clueless aid behind a desk, but the janitor was the one taking the trash out of the ward, and I felt very strongly that this janitor was more than a janitor. She was a beautiful woman I thought was an agent for the "good guys." To protect the janitor, I did not actually use the names of the thugs on my written notes. I wrote in code that I was sure the good guys would be able to understand.

What I'm realizing now, however, is that this psychiatrist who had been trying and trying to gain my trust over twenty years ago was not the enemy. I did not feel the necessity to let him in on what I was doing from 1987 to 1992, but at some level, I am convinced, he was on my side and wanted to help me and advance the cause of the good guys.

The preposterous loose association to which I have been referring involves my suspicion that this powerful big shot of a shrink may have taken a sperm sample from my body while I was under hypnosis in 1990. It would be the only opportunity he would have had to do so—to get a sample without me being aware of what had happened. I believe he may have been looking ahead and possibly based on something I said under hypnosis, concluded that such a sample might be the only way for me to become a parent. Circumstances might dictate that my unusual adulthood could keep me from being in a position to have children, especially if my eventual spouse was about my age.

The first memory I have after having been put under hypnosis is being given a cold dinner and told to get one night's rest with those candidates set to leave the base due to injury, etc. I was set to rejoin my platoon after spending one day in sick bay. Before going to sleep that night, I remember being on fire with desire for the female candidates who were talking with male candidates in a relaxed way. They were all anticipating going home. I was twenty-one years old, but I had never masturbated in my life up to that point.

I had only had nocturnal emissions. The flaming desire I experienced for the young women makes me suspect that a sperm sample may have just been taken from me while I was under hypnosis.

18

In chapter seven of this book, I state that I may now know someone who occupies a position both on my side of the wall and on the other side. I then state that the closest I've come to knowing someone who occupies both positions is the contact I had with my nemesis himself and his two cohorts. An exception to this idea is a worker on the psych ward I was sent to last summer for three weeks, the ward that was three hours away from my home. Sometimes I feel like I know this worker, because we experienced such a fulfilling connection during the three weeks. Sometimes I am convinced that he is a fellow counterrevolutionary, though I have no evidence for this suspicion.

At one point last summer, he brought me into my room on the ward and asked me pointedly if there was anything I felt I wanted to tell him, any information I wanted to impart. I took the opportunity to bounce off the man my suspicion that my 2006 blunder, when I sent my first book to a New York City scam, and what I felt probably happened as a result—the book falling into the hands of my nemesis—that this "unfortunate" occurrence may have been an act of leadership on my part. I explained that I may have had in mind the legal principle of "discovery," that the cause may have been advanced by both sides having access to the sensitive information in book one—that I had made 1992 identifications in a secure psych ward that had national security implications. The worker said meaningfully and without hesitation: "You are a leader, and you are a great thinker."

His response contrasts sharply to the one I received in 1996 or 1997, when I shared with a friend what I suspected I had been up to from 1987 to 1992 at the big state university. That friend asked me: "Now, Tim, do you really believe that you have had that big an impact on the things of this world?" I can't help being extremely resentful that this person responded to me in that way, because his response was one of the reasons I fell "asleep" in 1997, why I fell into an eight-year remission that I now call a re-mission. Part of the reason I am so resentful, of course, is that I purposefully avoided, during these eight years, movies or magazine interviews featuring WR, because I wanted to remain "healthy." Wilco's 2001 song, "I Am Trying to Break Your Heart," which appeared right in the middle of my time asleep, seems to me now to be referring to what WR must have been going through during the eight years of silence.

During the years 1996 and 1997, in what I now *know* were lucid moments, I had sent handwritten love letters to WR, which I sent through the care of another movie star, someone I don't think I need to conceal as to identity— Jodie Foster. I originally sent some of my writing to Foster's office in California, along with an envelope in which my writing could be returned. I received the writing back in the mail, with the explanation that the office cannot accept "unsolicited" work. But on the envelope, I received was an updated and quite different address stamped conspicuously in the upper left corner. I took this opportunity to send love letters sealed and labeled with WR's name to the address for Jodie Foster. I believe it is significant that when I sent the original unsolicited writing to Foster, I also included a small, red pin with the word *courage* on it and that the pin was not returned with my writing.

The reason I took the gamble that Jodie Foster was a member of the counterrevolutionary forces was her undeniably triumphant behavior at the Academy Award ceremony in the spring of 1992, which I watched on television while actually engaged in the domestic espionage at the big state university. She was on stage, with others, in 1992 accepting the award for Best Picture: *The Silence of the Lambs*. I believe that I learned much from viewing that movie more that once during the 1991–1992 school year. The fact that Foster, in the movie, appears before Anthony Hopkins as fresh meat to be devoured had in my mind unquestionably analogous meaning because I had spent the years 1988 and 1989, along with the spring of 1990, in counseling sessions with the man I now believe to be the cohort of my nemesis. The "strategy" I had developed, possibly from the age of six, involved trying to join the Marine Corps. I now believe that others in the counterrevolution made sure that I went head to head with a man suspected of being one of the principals in the assassination of President John Fitzgerald Kennedy, a man who had become an officer in the Marine Corps. It is the hallmark of my grandiose scenario that I was able to read the face of the suspected man, my Marine officer instructor, and make conclusions based on intuition. Actually serving active duty as a Marine myself became unnecessary because the next step in the espionage I was engaged in involved going after the other two principals, the other two people who actually pulled the triggers in the case, who were to be found, I felt, in the civilian realm. This left me the rather stupendous problem of heading for Marine Corps Officer Candidates School in June of 1990—a place which is supposed to cement in the initiate the idea of wearing a uniform—needing to return to my big state university as a civilian so that the other two suspects, which I believe I already had in my sights, would not be on their guard against a man about to become a Marine Corps officer. The idea is that I could similarly learn from the other two through intuition and make conclusions about the case. I had signed on the line, at the beginning of my sophomore year, committing myself to four years as an officer or two years as an enlisted man. My first two books are full of the drama that had been brewing in my life and that ensued when I made the trip to Quantico, Virginia, in June of 1990.

I have reason to believe that the counterrevolutionary forces in this country had in place measures that would have enabled me to "fake" mental illness as a means of escaping my commitment to military service so that I could continue the domestic espionage. What I have written about the hallucinations I supposedly saw on the psych ward in 1992, I also claim to be true of what I saw on the television in the acute care section of a clinic I found myself in after leaving Quantico in 1990. I believe the images were piped in from the outside.

But what surprised everyone is that I actually came down with a legitimate mental illness—as I experienced a nervous breakdown that involved five delusional episodes in which I was convinced that I had died and gone to hell. I believe that the psych ward worker I became close to in the summer of 2012 was an example of my "handlers" speaking to me directly, but this time through an actual person and not through images on a television.

19

It is always frightening to me: considering the prospect of publishing writing that suggests that an officer in the Marine Corps, now retired, was responsible for a heinous crime. The pill is not easier to swallow when I state that the crime must have been committed before the person became a Marine. It is also only marginally helpful to state that I believe the man was a suspect before I entered the picture in 1987 as a "spy." Indeed, I believe that I was pitted against the man intentionally, that the counterrevolutionary forces were hoping that I might be able to advance progress on the case, the case of the assassination of JFK. I have reason to believe that my nemesis was also a suspect in the case long before I began my work in 1987, but I was unaware of it. I state earlier in this book that I believe the little references and coincidences I have picked up on in movies, books, and music—those that encourage me—take the opposite form for my nemesis. I believe he sees items on an almost daily basis that persecute him with the idea that he has been found out in his guilt and that he may even one day be prosecuted and executed.

I have long since concluded, also, that the two cohorts in the case were merely henchmen—that it is my nemesis who was the brain involved. In the recent movie called *Page Eight*, the principle is mentioned: spies are never to reveal a piece of intelligence unless there is a reason for it. I have decided, therefore, not to say a word about cohort number two, even though I believe it was my contribution to the case to identify number two. I think the good guys had two suspects in the case but needed my help to arrive at a third.

I am convinced that the five delusional episodes I experienced during the ordeal I went through after flying from my home to Quantico in 1990 were actually my first experiences with bouts of paranoia. Because I had never experienced the feeling before, because I was in such stressful circumstances, and because my mood disorder had also introduced the problem of mania into the mix, I mistook the feeling for being in hell. I had collapsed with acute heat stroke at Officer Candidates School only a day or so before the first of the delusional episodes, so my logic concluded that I had died when I collapsed and that everything I had experienced after the heat stroke had been hell. I thought it was in character for Satan to have fun seeing the tormented person believe for a while that he was not in hell and then be sunk even more ruefully into the realization that he had been damned, even more ruefully than the last time, or the last round he had been through.

In my second book, I lobby hard for the idea that I had never actually slipped into psychosis in 1990, that my main reason for being so sure was that I *did* experience psychosis in the psych ward in 1992 and that the experience was nothing like what I'd been through at any point in 1990. I believe this point is important because I suffered greatly after experiencing psychosis in 1992, and it took me a long time to recover. I don't believe I could have returned to the spy business so quickly—in September of 1991—after only a year away from my big state university if I had experienced psychosis in 1990.

I must concede, therefore, that because of the highly sensitive nature of my work—whether it be the espionage or the writing I began to complete when I finished book number one in 2005—I may have to wait to be published. The small subsistence income I have mentioned is actually sufficient for my needs. I just yearn for the time in which I won't be so pent up and frustrated when it comes to being honest about what is on my mind.

The 1991–1992 psychiatrist who tried so hard to gain my trust during my touchstone year may have been anticipating that my adulthood might be lonely and unusual. While I did not let him in on what I had been up to from 1987 to 1992, I have no idea what I let him in on while I was under hypnosis in 1990. I believe it is possible that he may have taken a sperm sample, at the only time at which it could have been taken without my knowledge, because he had my best interests at heart.

WR is about my own age. I went eight years, 1997 to 2005, without contacting her or even believing that I had any legitimate connection to her. The two years of self-absorbed long letters I wrote to her fan mail address, early 2006 to early 2008, may have left her feeling hamstrung because I was walling her off because she was not Christian, even though the letters, at first glance, were declaring my affection and my commitment to her. I was very confused at the time and had no one with whom I could confide about my predicament.

In a recent issue of *Time* magazine, Gloria Steinem wrote in a short article about Sheryl Sandberg: "For a woman to be loved, she has to fail, and for a man to be loved, he has to succeed. That's what the gender police say, and it's inhuman and unfair to both men and women." I take comfort from what she wrote because I believe I "failed" by choosing to pursue my ex-wife instead of WR in January of 2011.

20

The Killers came out with a song called "Carry Me Home," on *Battle* Born, which came out in September of 2012. The first stanza refers, I believe, to my leaving the psych ward I was sent to in the summer of 2012, the one that was three hours from my home. I didn't want to be told everything at any point, by anyone, because I knew that I still needed to be kept an isolated variable. Because I suffer from a thought disorder that makes me paranoid without the proper amount of medication in my system, I came to believe very early in the psych ward stay that WR was torn between loyalty to me and love for someone I saw working in the ward. The young man I saw in the ward had thick hair and beautiful teeth, and I thought he looked like the stereotypical Beatnik. I came to believe that I was not "the one" she wanted.

"Carry Me Home" includes this line, "The morning dove sings/With two broken wings." I believe this is an allusion to a song, called "One Wing," on Wilco's 2009 album. Two lines from that song go like this: "One wing will never ever fly, dear/Neither yours nor mine, I fear." But that 2009 album had come out before I got married. The "fear" I was dealing with in 2012 was that I had little hope of still being attractive to WR. After all, I had married someone else. Perhaps this is one reason I jumped to the conclusion that she was in love with the handsome Beatnik working on the psych ward. I didn't think I was "the one."

The song's recurring words, "Carry me home," are appealing to me, to understate it. The song seems to refer to my attempt to once again approach romance with WR, but this time by writing this very book—the chapters of which I am convinced are passing under her eyes—instead of by sending long, self-absorbed letters. The long letters were characterized by my presuming that WR and I were already involved in a relationship, something I can now see as delusional. I believe that the "good guys" are getting the chapters of this book to her as they are being written.

The song seems to be encouraging me to be free from my fear. It seems to be saying, "Don't be afraid to publish the story." I believe that many, many people have worked to "carry me home," and I am eternally grateful.

21

Wilco uses the word, "hypnosis," early in their song called "Whole Love." I don't believe that this is just random chance. I was hypnotized in 1990, and I have no memory of what happened while I was in such a state.

The song includes these lines, "And I know that I won't be the last/Cold captain tied to the mast. When Wilco came out with *The Whole Love*, I was tied to my ex-wife, and I strongly suspect that my handlers knew what was only a hazy possibility in the back of my mind: that she was a double agent. As I've stated previously, the conclusion dawned on me before I bought Wilco's album and before The Killers came out with *Battle Born*, but it seems to me that the good guys were poised to do whatever they had to do to bring me out of peril.

I have never been on the telephone with WR, but Wilco sings a 2009 song called, "You and I," that goes, "However close we get sometimes/It's like we never met." Packed into the song, "Whole Love," is a prediction, I think, of how I would feel after having separated from my ex-wife. The idea seems to be that I would no longer approach romance with WR with presumption and arrogance.

I did not forget how to love when I got married. I made a tragic mistake. By the grace of God, I did know when the marriage was dead. I didn't know, initially, when it was wrong. But I don't feel forlorn and full of regret. This book is my attempt to show my "whole love." Even before meeting WR, I feel "whole."

22

This book has reached climax. The rest of it will be falling action. Today is February 4, 2014. I have been working at it since the summer of 2011 but have not advanced the text itself since September 25. Over the past few months, I have streamlined my life by changing the way I spend disposable income and by getting to the point at which I exist with no caffeine. I see my psychiatrist, the one I've had since my August, 2012 relapse, on February 18. She suggested the last time I saw her, about three months ago, that she might reduce my medication again on the eighteenth, which would be the fifth reduction since the 2012 hospitalization.

I was honest with her three months ago about the fact that I am addicted to caffeine and about the amounts I was typically drinking on "bad days." I honestly believe, however, that I am doing so much better and feeling so much stronger, mentally, than I was doing, for example, when I was in the process of finishing my second book in the summer of 2010. As I have painstakingly explained in this book, I have gone from conceptualizing the people in my life as orbiting around me to believing and acknowledging that those behind the wall in front of me are also on my planet. I have tried hard to allow, in this third untitled book, for the possibility that I am wrong about my loose associations and key suppositions. I am getting plenty of sleep without the influence of Ambien or any other sleep aid. I am no longer seeing the clinical psychologist for once-a-month psychoanalysis.

I concluded recently as a means of summary that I used to depend on the fact that I could count on caffeine to affect me in three ways: (1) it made me more optimistic; (2) it brought words more readily to my tongue; (3) it improved my posture. It was very discouraging, however, when my system became so saturated with the stuff that large amounts failed to produce much of an effect. Abstaining for a while always eliminated this problem of tolerance. Caffeine does not produce in me delusional thoughts or commitment to a fixed, false belief.

I suppose a question might arise as one is reading this book: "Why is it so necessary that I remain an isolated variable, insulated by the possibility that I am simply deluded?" I have a vague, hazy memory of something that I believe occurred in the fall of 1990 as I was waiting to be sent home after my first hospitalization at Walter Reed Army Medical Center in Washington, DC. I state in my first book that I left the hospital regularly, after I had been switched from the acute care ward to a "step down" one, and saw movies at the many cinemas in the area, that I saw one movie featuring WR as many as thirteen times. I have since concluded that I may have seen the movie as many as twenty-five times. The Department of Defense had been supplying to me a stipend for spending money. I have a hazy memory of someone near the entrance to the hospital—I really only remember a voice—poking fun at the number of times I'd seen the movie as I was returning from the cinema one night. How could such a person know which direction I'd taken, which cinema I'd gone to, which movie I'd seen? I remember immediately shoving what I'd heard to my subconscious, but why was this shove so necessary? If the answer had been in the recent past to enable me to be truly fresh meat while counseling with my Marine officer instructor back at my big state university, like Jodie Foster in the movie, *The Silence of the Lambs*, if the answer was to keep the "meat" fresh for the prospect of taking on suspects number two and three after returning to the big state university, then why is it *still* necessary—more than twenty years later?

The answer is that it may not be. Perhaps a reason that it may have been necessary from 1992 to now is that I am being viewed as a leader who will emerge from obscurity when the time is right. Perhaps it has been necessary in my mind for far too long. Perhaps I might have had a chance to be united with WR much sooner if I hadn't botched the romance so badly and seemingly wasted so much time. In any event, what I'm suggesting is that I may be in control of the timetable because people are looking to me for leadership. Perhaps this book, if it is published, will open Pandora's box.

My first roommate at the psychiatric ward to which I was sent in 2012 behaved in a peculiar manner when he would turn his head and say over his shoulder the letters of the alphabet: "*B, R; B, R.*" I found this extremely intriguing because when I subsequently learned his last name, I realized that it was identical to the last name of my first roommate in the dormitory at the big state university, except that my university roommate's last name started with the letters, "*BR,*" and my psych ward roommate's last name started with a *W.* This is the same kind of hint as the one in 1990, when I was returning to WRAMC from the cinema, except that in 2012, I did not shove the experience to the back of my mind. When I explained this coincidence to my psych ward roommate, he responded, "Kind of makes you wonder whether this whole thing has been *orchestrated.*" This is what I mean when I say that in years past I would marvel at the sheer complexity of what being "right" implied, why the eight-year-old inside me did not successfully surface until I was in my mid thirties, on July 18, 2005.

23

Sometimes eye contact can communicate what words cannot. Perhaps it would be more accurate to say that eye contact can communicate *more* than words can. I have two memories—one at the beginning of my freshman year at the big state university and one at the end—that stand as examples in my mind of this phenomenon occurring in my life.

The example that occurred at the beginning of the year I have already mentioned in the preface to this book, but I will now elaborate. I was sitting in a lecture hall full of five hundred students, and my professor, up on stage—the one who encouraged us at the end of the semester to yell out, "Science of behavior" if we saw him on campus in the years ahead—was talking about the concept of "true genius." He was saying that those in this very rare category are usually beautiful people, not scrawny little misfits with thick glasses, as the stereotype goes. He said that it is absolutely amazing what can be accomplished by those blessed in this way. No one is ever going to convince me that I was misperceiving what I remember: He seemed to be making significant eye contact with me, out of the five hundred students, as though he was trying to make a point. I have sensed in myself what took hold in my mind on July 18, 2005, and I don't think I will ever be persuaded otherwise. I see the eye contact that occurred in this context as the opening of my five years of action, the "domestic espionage" I have written about in this book. I see the experience as the official beginning of the mission I undertook as an eighteen-year-old.

As was the case with the two hints I mentioned in the previous chapter—the one in 1990 and the one in 2012—the eye contact in the 1987 psychology class seems to me to be an example of my handlers gently directing my path, but not so much so that I would be in danger of knowing too much, or looking like I knew too much when I counseled with my Marine officer instructor, the man I believe to be the cohort of my nemesis. I vividly remember acknowledging my psychology professor's eye contact with a knowing expression of my own but not dwelling on what had just happened. I relegated the experience to my subconscious until the day when I could relax and savor the gravy of victory after the mission had been successful.

There was a time, however, at the end of that freshman year when my subconscious emerged and asserted itself, when I attempted to ally myself with someone I trusted, someone I felt was a key player in what was unfolding on the grand stage, what was bouncing around in my head as

I kept in mind the big picture. Gunny, as he preferred to be called, the Marine Corps gunnery sergeant assigned to my big state university, had coached the rifle team. I had become one of the best shots on the team, and I wanted to express to Gunny what I thought of his excellent leadership and professionalism. He motioned me to a seat in his office, and I proceeded to say that I believed my Marine officer instructor had "taken someone out" with a rifle at some point in his life. In my first two books, I say that I then said "something" about the leaders slain in the sixties. In retrospect, I'm thinking now that it may have been only eye contact passing between Gunny and me that led me to remember mentioning the sixties. I *know* I remember the eye contact vividly. I do not know for sure that I said anything beyond my comment about my MOI having "taken someone out." Gunny responded by saying that the Marine Corps has the best screening process of any of the branches of military service.

I have never experienced any "eye contact" with WR. We have never met. There are very few times I even mention anything about her to the people in my life. This is surely a hardship, but not one to which I am unaccustomed. The brief exchange between Gunny and me, in addition to *one* time I mentioned what was on my mind to my sister in May of 1991, constitute the only times I revealed to anyone, from 1987 to 1992, what I felt I had been facing.

My military psychiatrist, in May of 1991, had cleared me to try going without medication, and I began to decompensate while staying with my sister and her husband. I composed a ten-page piece of writing at this time, based mostly on journal entries, that was very disturbing, and I spoke to my sister about wanting to send it to WR. If I had actually sent it to her, it would have been taking the concept of "leading with my ass" to an even worse extreme. I need medication for thought and mood.

I can't believe that I'm going to see on the Internet any concrete news of WR being involved romantically with someone else. I believe the chapters of this book are passing under her eyes as they are being written. But I have never gazed into her eyes. In the movie, *Page Eight*, the spy says that the job is about knowing who to trust. I trust Gunny. I believe that, when it comes to trusting WR, it has been all about a long, slow process within me, one that has had wrapped up within it a letting go of trauma and a profound experience of repentance. I sense something happening within me as I learn to take hope to the next level. I no longer feel estranged from WR. What I look forward to—in the spirit of hope—is seeing how much more there is to be found in her eyes.

24

I am beginning to be conscious of experiencing God's rest, what is described in the book of Hebrews in the Bible. It says in Hebrews that what was available to the Israelites in the Old Testament, when they were to enter the Promised Land, is still available to us today. I ended my second book believing that God wants to be included in the wrestling process that people go through when trying to discern right from wrong and when they are faced with whether or not to obey. I am now immersing myself in the concept of falling into the arms of Jesus, trusting Him in all things. This is liberating, especially at this time of my life, as I contemplate the prospect of possibly attempting to e-publish this book.

The psychiatrist I had during my touchstone year tried hard to extract from me some idea for how I was planning to subsist financially on my own. If I could have somehow glimpsed into the future at that time, I would have described to him how fulfilling my life is now, even though I receive disability income. I would have told him that I love to give back to society through my volunteer work at the drop-in center and through my writing, which I believe will one day be published and widely read.

In my late twenties and early thirties, I shoveled snow, milked cows, and delivered newspapers while disabled with a mental illness. In my mid and later thirties I went back to school to finish my undergraduate degree, served on advocacy committees, and spoke publicly about my experience with mental illness. Usually, the public speaking took the form of a NAMI program called In Our Own Voice. The speeches were divided into six sections: intro; dark days; acceptance; medication; coping; successes, hopes, and dreams. I think I can generalize when I say that my audiences thought, at most times, that I had not really conquered the stage of acceptance. This was because it became apparent that July 18, 2005 had been such a pivotal date for me that it it served as the demarcation point beyond which I could not be persuaded, even temporarily, that I was wrong on the whole about what I call the grandiose scenario. My beliefs were categorized, generally, as a fixed, false belief. Part of the reason I think this book is more palatable and publishable now than the other two books I've written, however, is that I am not taking refuge in the grandiose scenario in a way that renders my three-dimensional life unacceptable.

The concept of "rest" as a process of falling into the arms of Jesus may seem contradictory to a process of "wrestling," but what ties them together is what happens when a person is in the Word, the Word that is described in Hebrews as "living" and "active." One of the Bible studies I attend promises that the Word of God will always transform, regardless of how familiar one is with what one is studying. My parents recently gave me the NIV Bible on MP3, which allows me to hear, with my headphones, a narrator reading the text. The text also appears on a screen as the narrator is speaking.

Without caffeine in my system, I feel less inclined to talk to people about what I have been keeping secret in my mind. The words don't come readily to my tongue. It seems as though I am entering yet another phase of development, one in which I am content to keep my own counsel and be my best friend. This silence is, of course, what I have been accustomed to for most of my life, but I am perceiving in myself a sense of peace as I become more and more hopeful that I may have another "best friend" who is on my side and rooting for me all the way—WR. At the same time, I am becoming more and more conscious of Christ's invitation to take His "yoke" upon me and "learn" from Him. I guess I never fully realized before that if one is yoked to Christ, then one is always very near to Him, and that is such a comfort as I cope with my situation, which is unique to an extreme that borders on the ridiculous.

The previous paragraph I wrote yesterday has triggered an upturn in my mood and has brought about a resolution to a general sense of despondency I had been mired in for a few days. It seems that moving into a new phase now is just what I needed. Acknowledging that my behavior will be different in the immediate future—that I no longer feel a need to expand the number of people in my life who know about my story—seems to be appropriate. In fact, the idea emboldens me to predict that I can carry the momentum I've felt since yesterday and finish this book by next June. Today is Valentine's Day—February 14, 2014. I'm tagging along with my parents next June and making a trip to another state, where my sister lives with her family. My goal is to finish composition before I embark on that trip. In just a few days, I will meet with my psychiatrist and find out whether my medication will be reduced for the fifth time.

25

Part of the purpose of this book is to impart to the reader a measure of understanding as to what it feels like to be mentally ill—specifically—what it feels like to be me. I therefore feel inclined to delve further into what I am experiencing, now that my system is free of caffeine, now that I feel more and more convinced that this grandiose experience of mine cannot be "all in my mind."

The sensation I must admit I am trying to fight is another drop into feeling like I am in opposition to my reader. It seems sometimes to me that I have made this flop—with the significant exception: I am hoping that WR is hopeful that I will not be afraid anymore. When I make my way through each day that comprises my three-dimensional life, I am beginning to find that keeping silent about grandiosity immerses me in the minutiae and the detail that is concrete, and I am simply distracted for a while from thinking the thoughts I am happy to dwell on when I am alone. This delay or postponement of being the person I regard as whole makes me feel sometimes drained or exhausted. Living, as I am, with my parents exacerbates this problem because I have a tendency to want to spend my evenings in the living room where it is warm and where I enjoy their company. Watching the extensive coverage of the 2014 Winter Olympics on television is exaggerating what I'm feeling even more. I seem to need time to be the person I believe I am!

My psychiatrist reduced my medication for the fifth time since August of 2012. I'm hoping that as the weather warms up and as I am able to exercise more, I will spend more time out of the house, perhaps composing the remaining chapters of this book on my laptop computer. I'm sure that part of the attraction I associated with sipping caffeinated soda was simply being alone with my thoughts and enjoying the music on my MP3 player. I must admit that feeling as I do that I am not really alone when I am creating digitalized words on a word processor is something I have accepted as a given, concrete fact that I can't afford to doubt. But believing that the good guys are also tuning in makes me feel excited, as though I am leading the charge up a hill. Believing that WR is privy to what I'm writing is by far the biggest motivator I experience to keep going and be persistent, despite what I may be feeling when I make my way through the dry and thin reality I wrote about at the beginning of this book, when I was making my way through semester number seven. I am by no means saying that what is happening now is in direct correlation with the arid stretches I went through during semester seven of that touchstone year, but I perceive vestiges of the unwelcome feeling.

I wrote a newsletter article for the drop-in center today that reads as follows:

> It can be very confusing when considering the definitions for illusion, delusion, hallucination, and theory. I was once using a vacuum cleaner in a part of a church building that left me sequestered from others, and I "heard" what sounded like garbled voices speaking through a walkie-talkie that might be used by the military. When I turned the vacuum cleaner off, the voices stopped. I was very frightened because I have not been afflicted in my life with the phenomenon of hearing voices in one's head. Later I was relieved to learn that what I had experienced was an example of an auditory illusion brought on by the droning noise.
>
> While I haven't heard voices in my head, I have heard words from psych ward televisions that people tell me couldn't have been real. I was once in a coffee shop and heard on the TV news that it is now known that Robert Kennedy had been shot with two different weapons. Call me crazy, but I think that is rather significant. No one in the coffee shop could have cared less. Did I hallucinate the news story? Does the fact that I think the news is significant—and others don't seem to—make me crazy? In the end, what is real and what isn't? If I have become convinced that

certain things are true, or at least possible, and no one around me agrees, am I somehow duty-bound to somehow force myself to believe what doesn't make sense to me?

Because the newsletter will be copied and distributed, it occurs to me that I might be advertising the idea that I have grandiose beliefs, but I don't think I should be fearful of what may result. I talked to my friend tonight, the one who has published a book on the Internet, and he showed me a Web site with an article that said that an e-book that can be downloaded at no charge gets about one hundred times more hits than a priced e-book. I am seriously considering trying to e-publish this book that way—so that people could download it free of charge.

26

As I review what I have so far written in this book, it occurs to me that in chapter two I state that I began to suspect in 1997 that my nemesis was feeling paranoia, while in chapter eight, I state that it is my impression that he didn't realize that he was being "hunted" until after my 2006 blunder/ decision. This might seem something of a contradiction. Obviously, I do not know to what extent the good guys have been making the life of my nemesis miserable. I don't know when, or at what rate, the pressure and the paranoia mounted and increased. I don't know, of course, that I'm right about my nemesis being afflicted at all. But it is my suspicion that, from 1997 to 2006, the good guys had only been hinting to my nemesis that something was, for him, wrong in his life. I suspect that the wisps of paranoia took the form of an uneasy, uncomfortable feeling that led to my nemesis occasionally having the wild thought: "Surely my secret can't have been found out." In other words, I suspect that he was haunted with the wispy ghost of a doubt as to how secure he could feel.

After 2006, however, I believe that things changed dramatically. Not only did my nemesis now know that he was being hunted, but he knew who to blame and focus on when it came to his attempt to mount his counterattack. I'm not saying that I was the sole author of his troubles. Hardly. But he now had a focal point. He had a place to direct his attention and his energy.

One of the benefits of talking once a month to a clinical psychologist for six months was that he helped me with the idea of feeling more secure about the swinging of the power pendulum. I believe that the time has come and the point has been reached at which my nemesis has more to worry about than I do, because his ability to affect circumstances is going to decrease in the future more and more. Time is on my side. It says in the Bible that fear is about punishment. The song called "Be Still" by The Killers seems to me to be about being strong and steadfast, leading without fear, so that others can benefit.

The upside of my nemesis knowing that he was being hunted, I feel, was that the good guys no longer had to downplay their persecution. They could be blatant about it. I suspect that the movie *Ocean's 13* includes a scene in which Matt Damon enters a room with a small patch on his neck labeled "The Gilroy," because Tony Gilroy wrote and directed the movie, *Michael Clayton*, which I have said earlier seems to me to be a "call to arms." It seems likely to me that my nemesis has spent his fair share of time in gambling casinos, and *Ocean's 13* probably has many little references and "coincidences" that make my nemesis distinctly uncomfortable, or perhaps the reference to the Gilroy is blatant enough. Again, I have noticed hundreds of such instances over the past two decades in movies, books, and music—but for me, the items almost always build me up and encourage me. Even the criticism I processed in the lyrics of Five for Fighting, Wilco, and Finger Eleven seemed to appear in the spirit of hope, hope that I would rethink my position and open my mind.

When I say that the good guys were poised to bring me out of peril, the variable still needed to be isolated. I eventually sought out *The Whole Love* and *Battle Born*, something that was probably expected by those hoping to help me. No one knocked on my door and beat me over the head with the truth of the matter, what I had gotten myself into. It stood to reason that if I had noticed references in Wilco's music and in the music of The Killers in the past that spoke to my situation, then eventually I would pull my head out of the sand and check into the latest albums produced by these two bands.

There are three songs by the band called Linkin Park that deal with paranoia: "Papercut," "One Step Closer," and "Crawling." The overwhelming impression one gets while listening to these songs is that they are speaking about someone who is becoming more and more overcome with paranoia and fear, that this person can never fully escape the feeling and is "about to break" under the strain. This is what I mean when I say that my nemesis is in a prison with no walls. When I wrote my second book, I allowed for the possibility of his repentance, of his turning to God and seeking redemption. I made the point: Would it really be the best thing for him if God went easy on him and lightened the load, if God made his life easier to handle? "One Step Closer" features the singer screaming at one point in frustration: "SHUT UP WHEN I'M TALKING TO YOU—SHUT UP!" If I'm right about my grandiose beliefs, then the life of my nemesis must be almost unlivable.

27

I suppose one might question how I can state that I need medication for thought and mood and yet make the claim that the identifications I made in a 1992 psych ward should be granted a fair hearing and treated with credulity and even respect. After all, I went without medication from December 1991 to April 1992. The key to the answer is what I mentioned earlier in this book, when Amiri Baraka seemed to be trying to communicate with me when he stated at the beginning of his spring 1992 speech that he was taking lozenges to treat his sore throat because his speaking schedule was so taxing and strenuous. He repeated the comment at least three times as though he were emphasizing it on purpose, and I came away from the speech convinced that he was trying to say to me that I might have to take some of my medication if I was going to be successful with the espionage I was undertaking. It was a loose association and still left me an isolated variable.

Soon after hearing the speech, I began taking my medication again. I took it from April 1992 to the end of May 1992. But it is significant that I didn't begin taking it again until I was ready to leave campus to return to Michigan.

The seeming contradiction—that I can admit that without medication, my mind goes too far and comes up with absurdity, and yet while heavily medicated, I can still believe in the possibility of preposterous key suppositions and loose associations—is really not a contradiction at all. It is one of the foundations of my self-concept and can be summed up with the well-worn sentence: "There is a fine line between genius and madness."

My hope that a sperm sample might have been taken from my body in 1990 died hard. I can now admit that I don't believe it is true. But the fact that I needed evidence that it wasn't true is something I am not ashamed of. I think, under the circumstances, it was natural for me to cling to the possibility. *On the other hand, perhaps the "evidence" I "needed" is really the few sentences I just wrote. Perhaps I am trying to deal with the pain I am feeling.*

When I made the trip in the back of a police car to the psych ward in 2012, I was expecting to be taken to an auditorium full of admirers instead of a psych ward. Yes, this was absurd. During the night before the trip, I was convinced that my nemesis had wormed his way to a position in which he was the only person with the headphones on, that he was in charge of all gathering of intelligence for the country. Obviously, this was absurd.

I jumped to the conclusion that the handsome "Beatnik" working in the psych ward was a rival, only because he seemed competitive when he read some writing I had done during an early night on the ward. This was absurd. But all these absurdities I believed without any medication in my system. I crossed the line into madness.

But this is the factor that is penultimate because it explains how I can possibly believe that I could have done what I claim I did from 1987 to 1992: I needed to be a little mad to successfully make the loose associations I did, especially from December 1991 to April 1992. I would go on, in a psych ward in June of 1992, to not only theorize who the three assassins were, but to hypothesize which assassin was responsible for which shot. Indeed, I also theorized which of the three went on to assassinate Malcolm X, Martin Luther King Jr., and Bobby Kennedy. It was my belief that each one of the three was responsible for one of the subsequent assassinations after JFK was gone.

And here is where my little scrap of paper comes into play. On the paper, I wrote: "…about the truth of who I am, and how little that depends on whether I am right." When I experienced a schizophrenic reaction in the presence of the big shot of a shrink I was seeing in the spring of 1992, he asked, "How's the medication coming?" When I admitted that I hadn't been taking it, he became immediately concerned and asked how long it had been since I'd taken it. I lied and said, "Two weeks." He begged me to take it, saying that it is like a cast for a broken bone—put too much stress on it, and the bone will break. "And you may lose it."

And yet I flew from Michigan, still without medication, to spend one more week at the big state university. I rolled the dice one more time. The stakes were that high. I said to my mother at the airport, when I was about to depart, "If I should ever lose my sanity completely, take anything I write on paper to be a self-portrait." I meant that it wouldn't be me anymore. This took tremendous courage, whether or not I'm right. I had prayed to God about whether to take medication and sensed that I shouldn't. After the last week at the university, I began to take my medication again. I took it until the time came to rid myself of my big shot shrink, whom I had not trusted, and enter the psych ward in June of 1992. I can remember my older brother calling my dorm room the night before I left to return to Michigan and asking my roommate if I'd taken my medication. My roommate had answered, "Yes." I believe it was the first time I'd taken any since December. I can't account for how I had held together for more than three months without it. My behavior had been very strange, and I was constantly moving by instinct, but I did not cease to function. All I can say is that God had work for me to do and strengthened me.

28

I am not involved in a romance with someone I've never met. This seems like such an obvious thing to realize and acknowledge. Because of my beliefs about my life being so extraordinary, however, I needed evidence, once again, that it was true. Maybe I should write, "I am no longer involved in a romance with someone I've never met." The evidence that had me believing that romance was still a possibility, mostly perceptions from many years ago, I must admit now seems shaky and maybe not as reliable as it seemed in the past. Perhaps I was mistaken all the way along. So much of what I'm drawing from when I make grandiose conclusions I can't mention in a book. It is also important for me to remember, I think, that the good guys and the people I perceive as having "carried me home" do not dwell in one apartment in New York City. I think it is probable that The Killers, for example, may have been doing some speculating of their own when they came out with the song called "Carry Me Home." It certainly still seems to me that the lyrics in Finger Eleven's album, *Life Turns Electric*, which came out at the end of 2010, were attempting to bring about in me a change of heart. Perhaps a line from the song, "Stone Soul," is significant: "And if I ever make it back to you /Just know I wanted to."

I guess the glaring question is, If I had made the right decision in January of 2011, just how would I have gone about my attempt to pursue and woo someone I'd never met, even if there was evidence in the past of romantic interest? I admit that this almost has me stumped. Maybe it was another reason I made the decision I did. All I can say for certain is that by the fall of 2012, I imagined a sense of inevitability. I thought there was a biological link created by my psychiatrist/hypnotist having my best interests at heart when it comes to my becoming a parent.

Perhaps the supposition I have been clinging to is not valid. Perhaps the little ditty I heard in my apartment with the line, "You treat me like I've got green polka dots," was a hallucination after all. I guess my logic goes like this: I simply cannot discount all the references and "coincidences" that comprise my grandiose scenario, and if even one of them is real, then it opens the door for others being also reliable. What justified my hope in the biological link was a series of references in movies and music, which seems a lot less crazy if one believes, for example, that the movie, *Our Idiot Brother*, was inspired by my story.

With the recent decrease in my medication, I can feel my metabolism picking up. I am getting healthier in body, mind, and spirit. Even the newer antipsychotic medication tends to create and trigger weight gain, an increase in cholesterol, sluggishness, and a greater risk of diabetes. But the benefits outweigh the negatives. I wrote in chapter 16 of this book, which I have decided to title, *The Isolated Variable*, that the realization I made in chapter 13 was more traumatic than I thought at first. I have made a similar realization at the start of this chapter, but I am a lot healthier now.

Back at the start of 2006, eight years ago, I sent the first of the hundred-long, self-absorbed letters to the fan mail address of the woman I've never met. I showed a copy of this first letter to my former psychiatrist, the one I had for sixteen years. She immediately wanted to add a third antipsychotic medication to the two that had been prescribed for me since 1997. I agreed to take it. I believe that at some subconscious level, I knew that there was something wrong with what was in that first letter. I have always been praised for the insight I have into my illness. I am now on only two psychiatric medications, one for thought and one for mood. The one I have been taking since 1997 is currently at the lowest level in any of those seventeen years. I think this is appropriate, despite the fact that my grandiose scenario remains unshaken since July of 2005.

I am composing, at the moment, in the break room of the health club I joined last November. Today is March 17, 2014. When I made the realization I opened this chapter writing about, I thought at first that maybe I should relinquish my goal of finishing composition by the first week of June. But now I'm thinking that it should still be in effect. I have resolved to write an introduction for *The Isolated Variable* sometime between now and when I make the trip in June.

The winter of 2013–2014 has been very cold, and my father says that he read a prediction which stated that the next couple winters may be also long and frigid. In the past, I have not exercised as much during the winter because I usually relied on walking outside for exercise, and I didn't want to slip and fall on the ice or be hit by a car. I am consequently pleased with the fact that I now have a place to work out, regardless of what the weather brings. The drop-in center and the health club are now mainstays in what constitutes my three-dimensional day. I no longer look at it as being mired in the 3-D world.

29

Perhaps being delusional for such a long time (since July 2012) about having supposedly become a parent was beginning to wear me down a few weeks ago when I wrote chapter 25 of *The Isolated Variable*. The absence of caffeine in my system was probably making it harder for me to cling to the loose associations that produced the delusional idea. My desire to be alone with my music and dwell on what I perceived as the whole me was getting more and more difficult to do. It should not strike one as strange, however, that the delusion is now gone while I am taking less medication, that it was going strong even though I was on more medication in the fall of 2012. As this book painstakingly records, I was never convinced beyond any doubt. I chose to hope.

What the heavy doses of medication eliminated was the behavior that was present in the 2012 psych ward, when I was rude and commanding, utterly unlike my usual personality. The term that was used for the record was *assaultiveness*, and it markedly diminished gradually over the three weeks

I spent in the ward. The heavy doses brought me back to my true self, but I am getting healthier every day. I don't need as much medication as I previously did.

The psychiatrist I had for sixteen years was of the opinion that I was never fully in remission during the years 1998 to 2005. I know that I was *trying* hard to live without belief in the grandiose scenario. How successful I was is debatable I guess. When I wrote my second book, I concluded that I was actually in "re-mission," because I felt that I used the time period to marshal forces and take another run at my life goals and listen anew to what I perceived as my calling from God.

As I put more and more time behind me, I find that the number one goal I had for *The Isolated Variable*, to discern what should come next in my life, is coming to fruition. But what I'm discovering isn't anything like what I thought I would find when I started writing the book in the summer of 2011. I have concluded that the rest of this book should be a kind of springboard for book number four, that book number four itself is what should come next in my life, along with an even greater investment in my volunteer work at the drop-in center.

What I envision for my fourth book is autobiographical writing that does not become vainglorious. The Gospel of John records that at the time of Christ the point was made: testimony is not valid on the basis of only one witness. As the title indicates, *The Isolated Variable* is written from such a perspective. I have no one to corroborate my story. It is still my goal to finish composition before I make the upcoming trip with my parents, but I am now thinking that I will shelve the book much as I did when I finished my second book, when I only made five copies. I don't think I will try to immediately publish on the Internet.

Coming to this conclusion—that I should write a book that does not make grand claims about my place in the world—is a huge step for me, and I am amazed that the mental adjustments are coming so quickly. Today is April 3, 2014. The goal for book four will be to think from the standpoint that I am right about the grandiose scenario but not write from that standpoint. My first two books and *The Isolated Variable* have been immeasurably helpful to me from a therapeutic perspective, and I still believe that all three will one day be published, perhaps with footnotes. I think it will be viewed generally as valuable: my attempts to characterize the situation at different ages and at different times of my life. I'm sure there will be more of that in book four, but I hope to write between the lines of what has taken place before, which has essentially seemed, perhaps, raw and coarse.

I've said earlier in this book that the audience for my first two books was basically me. I suppose that is also true for this one. I have been trying to carve out for myself a definition of who I am. I think it is highly ironic that the conviction I feel very recently about being right about the grandiose stuff, the growing sense of peace that comes from no longer feeling conflict within me, is coinciding with the moment I resolve to refrain from writing openly about these very beliefs.

One concrete way this change is playing out is that I no longer hide spelling and grammatical errors when I use a word processor. I'm not totally sure why I ever chose to work this way before, but I think the reason has something to do with what I'm writing about now. I think I wanted my work to stand as some kind of historical document, mistakes and all. If this sounds conceited, I can only say that I have been conscious of a great man complex for as long as I can remember. The question I used to live with was, "Should I be ashamed of this?" The question disappeared on July 18, 2005, and the answer was a resounding "NO!" I recently heard myself saying to someone: "Everyone's life is extraordinary." I suppose this realization came a little late for me.

30

One of the climactic events that occurred in my life was Marine Corps Officer Candidates School in Quantico, Virginia—which usually happens after three years of undergraduate work as a Naval ROTC midshipman. It was a crisis point for me for a number of reasons. The Killers begin a 2008 song called "Human," with the lines, "I did my best to notice when the call came down the line. Up to the platform of surrender, I was brought but I was kind." It is my contention that I felt I needed to be a civilian in order to go after suspects number two and three in the JFK assassination case, that I had signed on the line committing myself to military service two years before, and that this created a crisis. But I believe I also had a less practical problem of reconciling the two opposing sides of the plank resting on the fulcrum that was Marine Corps OCS. On one side was the calling of the Christian to be a servant, to take upon oneself a cross and offer up one's body as a "living sacrifice." This involved an implication of humility and not thinking of oneself more highly than one ought. On the other side was what was taking more and more concrete form in my twenty-one-year-old mind, that I might have been shouldering—at the time—the titanic responsibility put to music in the form of the 1984 London musical *Chess*, that my role was to win a world-scale chess match, that I might have been the chosen one to accomplish this, and that I might have been chosen at the age of nine. I don't think it is a coincidence that the 2013 movie, *Ender's Game*, begins with the words, "Fifty years ago." Fifty years before the movie came out in the cinemas, JFK was assassinated in 1963.

So the question, "Should I be ashamed of myself?" for having a great man complex for as long as I can remember—reached a point of critical mass at OCS. Once again there were two sides of a plank resting on a fulcrum, which this time took the form of the moment I collapsed with acute heat stroke after the first three mile run and found myself in a large tub of ice water, wearing only a jock strap. On one side was the merciless self-recrimination I put myself through as I reviewed and remembered what I felt had been irresponsible incompetence as a midshipman back at my big state university. This lasted for several days, starting with at least three nights with no sleep at all, and ending with the three-mile run. On the other side was the sense of relief I felt as I floated in the ice water, which felt lukewarm, as my brain was put through many tests for damage at a hospital, as I was put under hypnosis, and as I spiraled from sick bay to a clinic and ultimately to Walter Reed Army Medical Center in Washington, DC. During this period of relief, it eventually dawned on me that I had gotten through the OCS experience, without quitting, having no commitment to serve in the military and no requirement to pay back scholarship money. The great man complex had reached a new level in my consciousness, and I began to plan for my last year at university, the touchstone year I began *The Isolated Variable* writing about.

Embodied by the fictional demon named Perfect, I had lived from age ten to twenty-one burying the concept of my own sinfulness rather than confessing it to God. This had led to my anguished psyche concluding that for me to have believed, at any level of consciousness, that I was primed to become the kind of hero heralded by *Chess*, was punishable by eternal damnation, and I experienced five delusional episodes during which I thought I was in hell. I couldn't reconcile the enormity of my role for good in the world with what I subconsciously felt about my failure to confess my sins as a Christian and how bad this made me feel about myself. Writing my first book helped me begin the healing process that didn't really end until I could write, at the end of my second book, that God removes sin "as far as the east is from the west." OCS happened in the summer of 1990. I didn't finish my first book until 2005, and I didn't finish the second until 2010.

I have said that my 2006 blunder/decision put book number one into the hands of my nemesis and that I suspect what I type in digital form is under review by both sides. I have to conclude, therefore, that my second book might also have been seen as it was being written. If this is true, however, then my first book was only seen as it was taking shape by the good guys. On the other hand, if the OCS hypnosis had triggered an FBI agent monitoring me in 1991, then perhaps there have been neutral guys also privy to what I have been writing. I have a gut feeling that it was of vast significance and importance that I kept my mouth shut while under the care of my touchstone year psychiatrist—perhaps even as vast as the ambitions the man seemed to have for me and my future.

The sense of conviction I am feeling at this moment of composition of being on the right track with my grandiose ideas is quite close to unparalleled in my experience. The pressure is off my back—the pressure that came with the prospect of publishing almost immediately. Perhaps I needed this release in order to be comfortable with what is yet to come with the chapters of this book.

31

I must admit that what I am experiencing as this book is ending is a recession of grandiose thoughts to the back of my mind, or to a deeper level of my consciousness. The last time I can recall that happening was the fall of 1997, the beginning of what can arguably be called my remission. The difference, however, is that losing the preoccupation in 1997 left me devastated and without any foothold on my concept of self, while today I feel a quiet confidence and a sense of conviction that I must simply wait for the Lord, whether or not that involves being right. A poem by an unknown author called "Answered Prayer" has become a treasure to me, and it reads as follows:

> He asked for strength
> that he might achieve;
> he was made weak that he might obey.
> He asked for health
> that he might do greater things;
> he was given infirmity

that he might do better things.
He asked for riches
that he might be happy;
he was given poverty that he might be wise.
He asked for power
that he might have the praise of men;
he was given weakness
that he might feel the need of God.
He asked for all things
that he might enjoy life;
he was given life that he might enjoy all things.
He has received nothing that he asked for;
all that he hoped for.
His prayer is answered.
He is most blessed.

Perhaps I will begin another period of re-mission, in which I devote myself to study of the Bible. That's what happened from 1997 to July 18, 2005. But I can remember the exact moment I "fell asleep" in 1997 and concluded that surely my mind had gone too far with its dreaming and ambition and childlike faith. My subconscious housed the grandiose scenario from 1997 to 2005, keeping it safe. In the front of my consciousness, the exact moment occurred while I was making a recording of my voice on cassette tape. I can remember saying the words into the machine: "I'm falling asleep. I can *feel* it." After I said those words, a curtain fell in my mind, and what had been accessible and easily retrieved suddenly felt a million miles away. I was left feeling bereft and forlorn.

I heard a sermon by my little brother's pastor that suggested that Christians should never, ever say to themselves: if only such and such were true, then life would be so much better. Thinking of winning the lottery, for example, he said should never be considered this way. His point was that if one has the treasure of salvation and redemption through the blood of Christ, then there is nothing that compares with such a life.

The grandiose scenario has shifted, it would seem, to a less prominent place in my life, but this time its elements do not feel millions of miles away. The prospect of writing book number four with quiet confidence is exciting to me. It stands in my mind as what should come next in my life.

32

There have been two occasions over the past few months when I have lapsed—drinking large amounts of caffeine. One was March 23, and the other was April 23. I am not proud of myself, and I hope that I won't give in to temptation in the future. I'd like to remain caffeine free for the rest of my life. I think it is useful, however, to compare the two mistakes.

On March 23 I was at an especially low point when I started to drink the caffeinated soda, and I began to almost immediately experience optimism about my future place in the world. The Killers sing, "Be still, and go on to bed—nobody knows what lies ahead." As my three-dimensional world asserted itself over the next few days, my optimism drooped without more caffeine, and I became very depressed and sluggish for several days. I felt like Pavlov's dog encountering a negative stimulus as a consequence to my behavior.

On April 23 I was in an especially good mood when I chose to once again step over the precipice and risk more punishment. This time my mind looked backward, not forward, and I began to experience affirming and rewarding confidence about past decisions and critical moments of my life. I would hope that my lasting abstinence from caffeine might be based on principle and not on fear of punishment. Today is April 24, 2014. I did not sleep last night, and even though I came to some moments of clarity while awake, I can see how destructive to my health drinking caffeine would eventually be, especially if I drank it on a regular basis, as I have in the past. I suspect that I am not on the verge of another tailspin into depression, but nevertheless, I am determined to make yesterday's lapse my last in this particular area of less than desirable behavior.

I am reminded, however, once again of Romans 8:28 (NIV): "And we know that in all things God works for the good of those who love him, who have been called according to his purpose." The difference between the two days, one month apart, fills me with hope and excitement. God can work even through my failings, and I believe He has in this case. I feel grounded and confident that I have not failed in life, despite the fact that I am forty-five years old with no children or spouse. I am doing what I have always wanted to do—spend a large portion of my time writing, and I am doing what always seemed out of reach when I was young—attending and even presiding over meetings, where much of the work goes on between my ears as a volunteer.

I have tried to live by principle and make my life a work of art. There have been many times in which my instincts seemed to have taken over, and I don't even remember making much of a conscious decision to go a certain way or pass up an opportunity. There have also been times I have felt the Holy Spirit taking over, and once again, I don't remember initiating or moving from my own sense of will at all. Words have come out of my mouth without my fully understanding from where they really originated.

It is when it comes to relationships with people, I suppose, that regrets make more of an entrance. But as I said earlier in this book, I no longer live with the fear that friends who have spent quality time with me can never be replaced. The Killers sing, "From here on out, friends are gonna be hard to come by." The isolation of being the isolated variable has been, over the years, intense at times. What I hope for from the future may be lacking in concrete terms and clearly defined parameters, but when it comes to how happy I feel most of the time and how joyful I feel nearly all of the time, I can't help but expect to connect on a rich and fulfilling level with people I love and welcome into my life. They may be hard to come by, but I believe I will find them.

The obstacle, of course—at least since July 18, 2005—has been, How can I be truly honest with people about who I am? How can I be silent about such a large part of my life? I can think of at least one friend who pretty much deserted me after this mystical date. Once again, I am reminded of my overriding purpose for *The Isolated Variable*: to discern what should come next with my life. My upcoming plans for book four answer the question more than adequately. I'm going to attempt to write an entire autobiographical book being essentially silent about this large part of my life.

I told a woman the other day, a woman who is currently reading my second book, that I hope to remain in the here and now with book four, and she responded warmly and enthusiastically. Perhaps I can expect a similar response from future potential friends, even if I must refrain from being truly honest with them. I suppose the quandary I am in at the moment is addressed by the song by Linkin Park called "Somewhere I Belong." The line goes, "I WILL NEVER BE/ANYTHING TIL I BREAK AWAY FROM ME." Much of the angst I associate with this song pertains, I believe, to what is contained in my second book and what I conclude at the end of that book, that God removes sin "as far as the east is from the west." But the quest, for me, remains. I must "break away."

Soli Deo gloria!